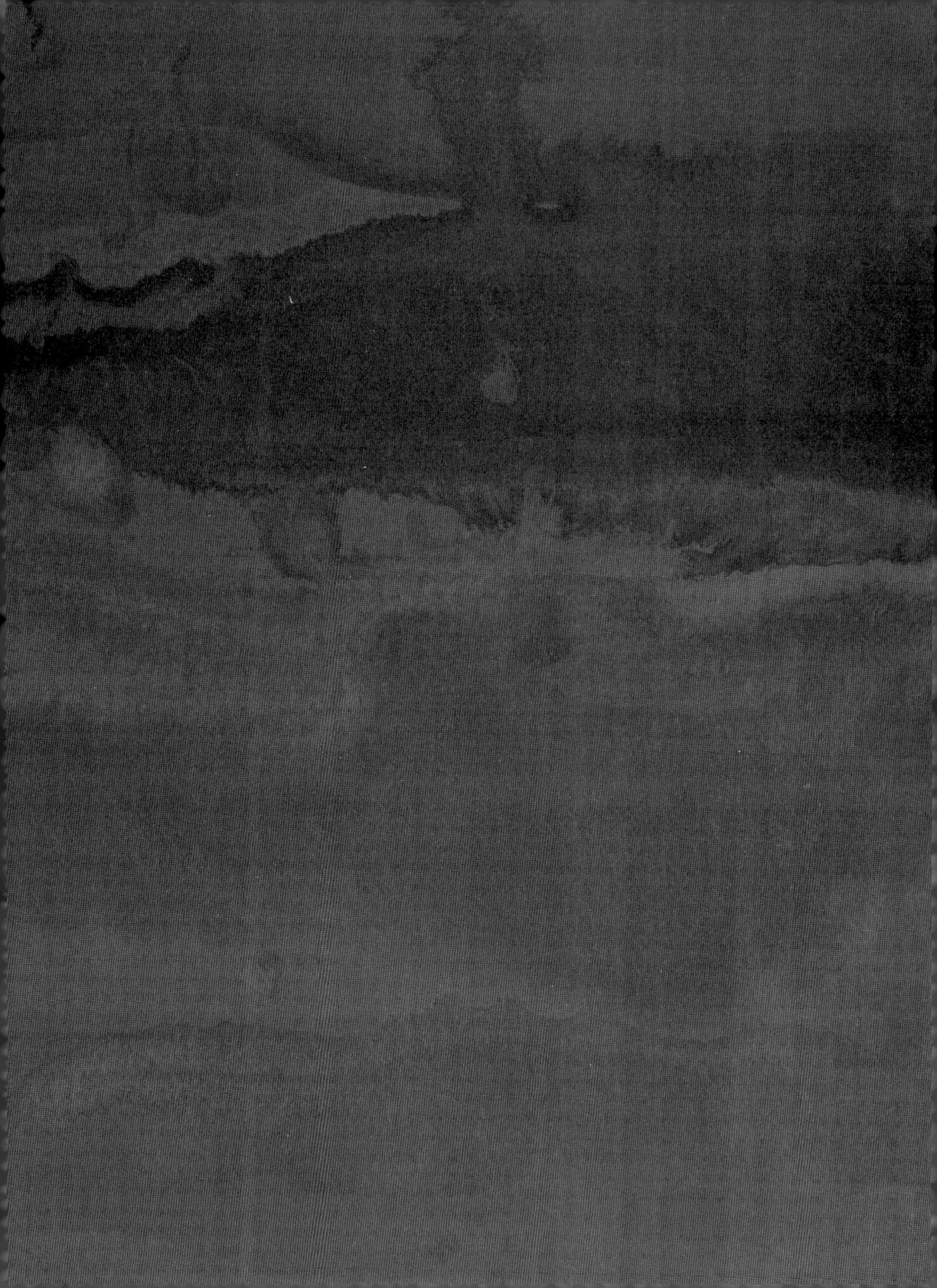

성웅 이순신,
한글로 기억되다.

Sacred Hero Yi Sun-sin,
Remembered in the Letters of Hangul

프롤로그

데칼코마니처럼 작업의 시작은 그가 되어보는 것이다. 관련 서적을 읽고 관련된 곳을 가보고 관련된 영상물들을 보며 눈을 감아보는 것이다.

젖은 발로 아무도 없는 해변가를 느리게 걷듯이 그가 되어 그의 생을 걸어보는 것이다. 손에 무언가가 잡히고 바람이 가져오는 소리가 들리고 무언가가 밀려와 호흡이 빨라지기도 한다. 묶인 매듭처럼 가슴이 묶여있다 풀리며 눈물을 동반하기도 한다. 감은 눈 속에는 무한의 세계가 있다.

'오래전'에 머문다. 산과 흙과 물과 공기, 그 사이에 꽂혀 있는 시간들, 돌돌 말려 있는 화선지 위로 그의 생이 펼쳐져 나온다.

남산 밑에 충무로와 청계천을 그리고 사이에 기와집을 넣는다. 이것이 이순신 장군 일대기의 시작 '탄생'이다.

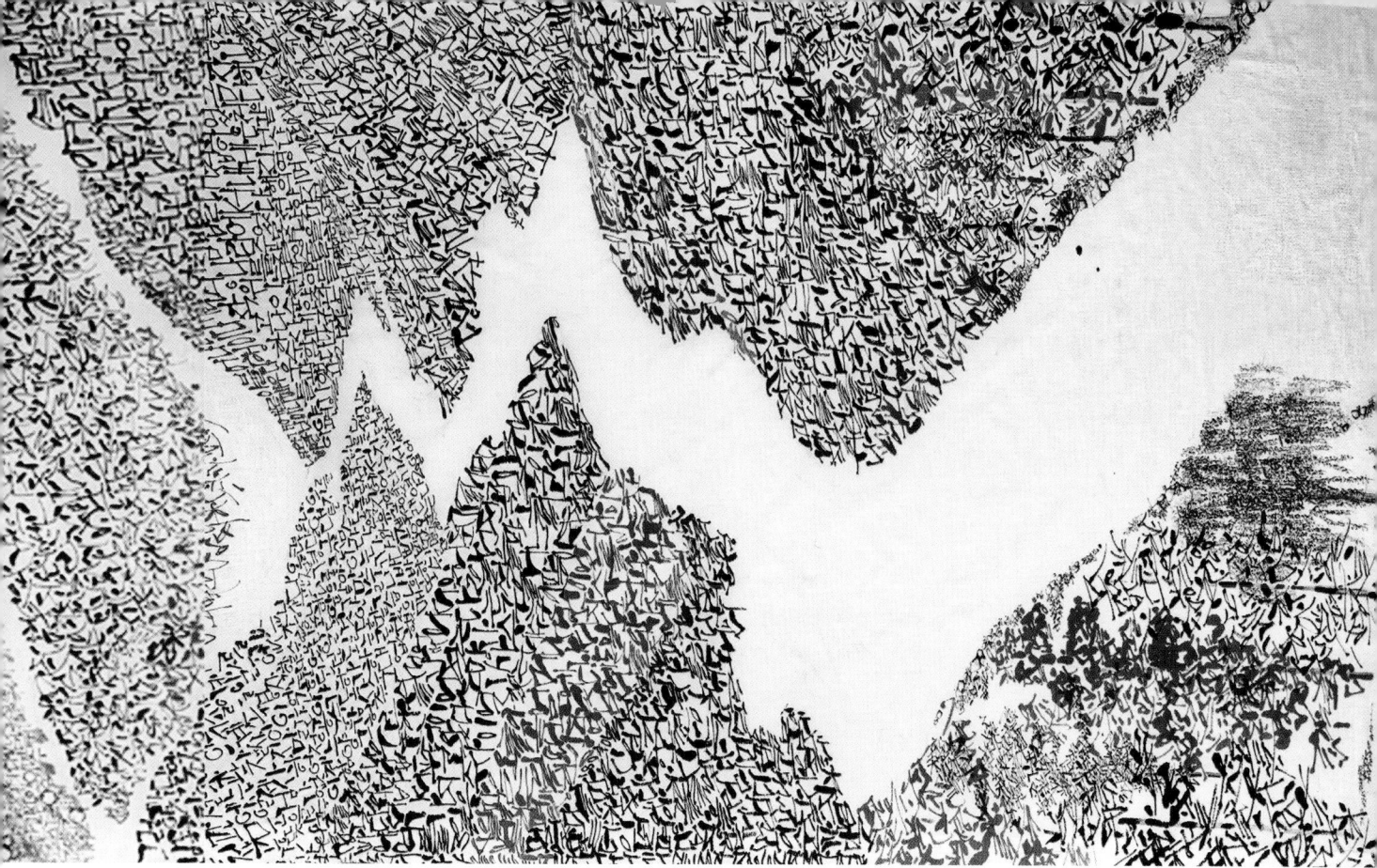

작품 위로 새들이 봄을 가져오고 구름이 산자락을 훑고 올라갈 때 엄마를 따라 외갓집으로 간다. 마당에는 쨍하게 반짝이는 빛과 그림자, 다정을 꿈꾼다.

다정은 서로의 마음을 내비치는 것, 이렇게 두 번째 작품을 이으며 나의 작업은 실타래처럼 저쪽에서 이쪽으로 옮겨오며 쌓여 간다. 자그맣게 쓰이는 한글이 나무가 되고 바람이 되고 동무가 되고 그리움이 된다.

점들이 더해지며 작품이 되는 점묘화처럼, 글자들이 모여 풍경이 되고 문장이 되어 이순신의 생을 말한다. 말하는 작품이 된다. 차분하고 따뜻한 성정, 불굴의 의지, 아랫사람에 대한 예(禮), 부모에 대한 효(孝), 나라에 대한 충(忠), 밤을 지새우는 고독… 효(孝)·충(忠)·예(禮)·인(仁) 그를 이루고 있는 사상들이 흐르고 흘러 여기에 와 닿는다.

한글로 그리는 이순신 장군의 일대기
'세종과 충무공의 만남'이라 일컬으며 스토리를 그려 나간다.

우리나라 사람이라면 모두가 사랑하고 존경하는 위인인 이순신 장군과 세종대왕, 나는 이들의 사랑을 받으며 때로는 애절하게 때로는 고통스럽게 몇 개의 계절을 보낸다. 귀하고 아름다운 작업을 할 수 있는 기회에 감사하며,

역사를 그리며
'바람이 바뀔 수도 있겠습니다'라고 쓴다.

– 서미숙

In preparing for the exhibition and publication of Admiral Yi Sun-sin's life story, the first step is to become him. Like a decalcomania print, the work begins by stepping into his world—by reading books, visiting places connected to him, watching films about his life, and then closing one's eyes.

It is like walking slowly along a deserted, wet shoreline—becoming him and walking through the course of his life. Something touches your hand, the sound of the wind carries to your ear, something swells within you until your breath grows heavy. At times your chest feels bound like a tightened knot, only to loosen with tears. Behind closed eyes lies an infinite world.

I dwell in the realm of 'long ago'—among mountains, earth, water, and air—where time stands suspended, and his life unfurls across a roll of white paper.

At the foot of Namsan, I sketch Chungmuro and Cheonggyecheon, placing a tiled-roof house between them. This is the beginning of Admiral Yi Sun-sin's life story: his birth. Above the canvas, birds bring spring and clouds sweep over the mountain slopes, as he follows his mother to his maternal home. In the courtyard, light and shadow shine brightly, and tenderness takes root as a dream.

Tenderness is the revealing of one's heart to another. With this, the second piece is joined, and my work accumulates thread by thread, carried from there to here. The small strokes of Hangul become trees, become wind, become companions, become longing.

Like a pointillist painting, where dots gather to form an image, here the letters come together to form a landscape, to weave sentences, to tell the life of Yi Sun-sin. The work begins to speak. It speaks of his calm and gentle nature, his indomitable will, his courtesy toward subordinates, his filial devotion to parents, his loyalty to the nation, his lonely vigils through the night... Filial piety (孝), loyalty (忠), propriety (禮), benevolence (仁)—these principles that shaped him flow endlessly until they reach this place.

This is Admiral Yi Sun-sin's life story, painted in the strokes of Hangul—a story I call **'The Meeting of King Sejong and Admiral Yi.'**

For all Koreans, Admiral Yi Sun-sin and King Sejong are figures of deep love and respect. With their presence, I pass through seasons—sometimes with aching sorrow, sometimes with pain. I am grateful for the precious and beautiful opportunity to create this work.

As I draw history,
I write: *'Perhaps the wind may yet change.'*

- *Mi Sook, Seo*

한글로 그린 역사 회화
20점의 작품이 이야기를 전개해 나갑니다.

History Painted in Hangeul
Twenty works unfold a story, piece by piece.

작업 과정 영상 보기

뿌리 : 삶의 시작과 길을 정하다

The Root – The Beginning of Life and the Chosen Path

이순신의 출생
Birth of Yi Sun-sin

   이순신 장군은 조선시대 한성부 건선동 지금의 서울 중구 인현동(서울특별시 중구 을지로 18길 19 신도빌딩 터) 남산 밑에서 태어났다.

   남산은 대한민국의 수도 서울특별시에 있는 해발 270m의 단단한 화강암으로 이루어져 있는 산이며, 중구와 용산구의 경계에 자리잡고 있다. 북한산, 인왕산, 안산, 관악산, 청계산, 대모산, 아차산, 불암산, 수락산, 사패산, 도봉산 등이 남산을 중심에 두고 요새를 지키듯 바라보며 감싸고 있고, 남쪽으로는 시간과 함께 한강이 유유히 흐른다.

   1545년 4월 28일 새들이 봄을 데려오고 구름이 산자락을 훑고 올라갈 때, 이 곳 남산 밑 마을에서 산의 정기를 받고 세계적인 명장이자 우리 국민이 가장 존경하는 위인, 충무공 이순신이 아버지 이정과 어머니 초계변씨의 셋째 아들로 태어난다.

   이순신 생가터는 아쉽게도 세월과 개발의 변화에 묻혀 자취는 남아 있지 않고 현재는 신도빌딩이라는 조그만 건물이 자리 잡고 있다. 나지막한 건물들과 좁은 골목길, 이따금 오가는 사람들, 빌딩에 붙어 있는 스티커들, 비스듬히 기울어져 있는 오토바이가 지금의 생가터 풍경을 이루고 있다.

   생가 부근에는 조선시대 무과시험을 치렀던 훈련원이 있어, 어린 이순신은 무관들의 훈련원 생활을 보며 자랐다. 총명하고 당찼던 이순신은 아이들을 모아 대장 노

릇을 하며 군사놀이를 하곤 했다. 한 일화로 아이들에게 지시하여 진지를 구축하고 전쟁놀이를 준비하던 찰나 한 어른이 길가의 진지를 밟고 지나가자, 이순신은 어른 앞으로 다가가 활로 눈을 겨냥한 뒤 "군사 진지를 어찌 함부로 지나간단 말입니까!" 하며 화를 냈다고 한다. 군사들이 훈련하는 모습을 보며 자연스럽게 무인의 삶과 익숙해졌으리라.

—

Admiral Yi Sun-sin was born beneath Namsan, in Geonseon-dong, Hansung-bu of the Joseon Dynasty—today's Inhyeon-dong in Jung-gu, Seoul (the site now occupied by the Shindo Building on Euljiro 18-gil).

Namsan, rising 270 meters above sea level, is a solid granite mountain at the heart of Seoul, the capital of Korea, lying on the border between Jung-gu and Yongsan-gu. Encircling it like guardians are the city's ring of mountains—Bukhansan, Inwangsan, Ansan, Gwanaksan, Cheonggyesan, Daemosan, Achasan, Bulamsan, Suraksan, Sapaesan, and Dobongsan. To the south, the Han River flows gently, keeping pace with the passage of time.

On April 28, 1545, as birds heralded spring and clouds brushed along the mountain slopes, Yi Sun-sin was born in this village beneath Namsan. He was the third son of Yi Jeong and Lady Byeon of the Chogye clan. From the very beginning, he was imbued with the mountain's spirit, destined to become not only a world-renowned commander but also one of the most respected figures in Korean history—known to the people as Admiral Yi, the 'Loyal Hero of the Nation.'

Sadly, the site of Yi Sun-sin's birthplace has long disappeared under the changes brought by time and urban development. Today, a modest building, the Shindo Building, stands in its place. Narrow alleyways, low buildings, the occasional passerby, stickers plastered on the walls, and a slanted motorcycle leaning by the curb form the current landscape of this historic spot.

Near his birthplace once stood the Hunryeonwon*, the military training ground where candidates for the state military examinations were tested. Young Yi grew up watching the lives of soldiers there. Bright and spirited, he often gathered neighborhood children to play war games, naturally assuming the role of commander. One well-known anecdote tells of Yi leading his friends to build a makeshift fortress. Just as they were preparing for their mock battle, an adult happened to step over their fortifications. Yi boldly confronted the man, pointing an arrow at him and scolding, "How dare you trample over a military stronghold!" Such childhood moments, spent in the shadow of soldiers and their drills, must have nurtured his early familiarity with the life of a warrior.

***Hunryunwon** The Royal Military Training Center of the Joseon Dynasty

탄생 *Birth*

남산과 중구와 이순신
Namsan, Jung-gu and Yi Sun-sin

아산시 소재 외갓집
Birth of Yi Sun-sin

많은 사람들이 이순신 장군의 출생지를 아산으로 알고 있는데 이곳은 외갓집이다. 이순신의 어머니는 초계변씨 수림의 딸이었으며 친정이 충남 아산 고을 백암리다. 이순신이 약 10~12세(추정)사이, 집안 형편의 어려움으로 인해 어머니는 식솔들을 데리고 서울에서 아산 친정으로 이주를 한다. 초계변씨 집안은 지역사회에서 상당한 재력을 유지하고 있었다.

현재 외가의 고택은 아산 현충사 내에 자리 잡고 있으며, 햇빛이 쨍하게 내리쬐는 마당은 눈이 부시고 세 그루의 나무들은 다정하게 개화를 꿈꾸고, 집 뒤로 울창하게 우거진 나무들은 집을 지키는 수호수들 같다. 집에서 느껴지는 온화하고 포근한 느낌과 터가 높지 않은데도 시원한 시야, 이렇게 평온하고 아득한 느낌은 이순신의 품성에도 자연스럽게 스며들었으리라.

이순신은 소년 시절을 이곳 외갓집에서 보내며 회신과 요신형들을 따라다니며 시를 쓰고 글을 배웠다. 무인의 기질도 다분하여 활쏘기와 말타기도 즐겨하며 문인과 무인의 자질을 갖추어나갔다.

이순신은 어려서부터 성격이 대범하여 주변에 억울한 일을 당한 사람이 있으면 가해자를 찾아 반드시 사과시키고 마는 사람이었다. 성장하면서 글을 읽어 큰 뜻을 깨달았고, 서법에 정통하였으며 사람됨이 용모가 바르고 신중하며 항상 근신하는 선비와 같았다.

Many people believe that Admiral Yi Sun-sin was born in Asan, but in fact, Asan was his mother's hometown. His mother, Lady Byeon of the Chogye Byeon clan, was the daughter of Byeon Surim, and her family home was in Baegam-ri, Asan, Chungcheongnam-do. When Yi was about 10 to 12 years old, due to financial difficulties, his mother moved the entire family from Seoul to her natal home in Asan. The Chogye Byeon family at the time maintained considerable wealth and influence within the local community.

Today, the old family house stands within the grounds of Hyeonchungsa Shrine in Asan. Its courtyard, dazzling under the bright sunlight, is graced by three trees that seem to dream of blooming together in harmony. Behind the house, dense groves of trees rise like guardians, protecting the home. Despite the modest elevation of the site, it offers an open and refreshing view. The gentle, warm, and serene atmosphere of this place must have naturally seeped into Yi Sun-sin's character.

Yi spent much of his boyhood at his maternal home, following his cousins Hoe-sin and Yo-sin, learning to read and write poetry. At the same time, he showed a strong inclination toward martial pursuits, enjoying archery and horseback riding, thus developing both literary refinement and military skill.

From a young age, Yi displayed a bold and upright nature. If he saw someone wronged, he would confront the offender and make sure they offered an apology. As he grew older, he studied diligently and came to understand great ideals. He excelled in calligraphy, carried himself with upright dignity, and lived with caution and discipline, embodying the character of a true Confucian scholar.

Sadly, the site of Yi Sun-sin's birthplace has long disappeared under the changes brought by time and urban development. Today, a modest building, the Shindo Building, stands in its place. Narrow alleyways, low buildings, the occasional passerby, stickers plastered on the walls, and a slanted motorcycle leaning by the curb form the current landscape of this historic spot.

Near his birthplace once stood the Hunryeonwon*, the military training ground where candidates for the state military examinations were tested. Young Yi grew up watching the lives of soldiers there. Bright and spirited, he often gathered neighborhood children to play war games, naturally assuming the role of commander. One well-known anecdote tells of Yi leading his friends to build a makeshift fortress. Just as they were preparing for their mock battle, an adult happened to step over their fortifications. Yi boldly confronted the man, pointing an arrow at him and scolding, "How dare you trample over a military stronghold!" Such childhood moments, spent in the shadow of soldiers and their drills, must have nurtured his early familiarity with the life of a warrior.

아산 외갓집 *Yi's Maternal House in Asan*

빈궁과 영달은 오직 하늘에 달렸으니

모든 일은 모름지기 자연에 맡겨두라

부귀함은 때가 있어 홀로 차지하기 어려우며

공명이란 임자없이 번갈아가며 전해지는 것

마땅히 천천히 갈 때는 천천히 걷고

처음에 먼저 오를 때에는 넘어질 것을 염려하라

티끌세상 헤치며 나아가는 길에

남의 뒤를 가더라도 채찍질은 하지 마라

– 이순신이 청년 시절에 쓴 시
〈충무공 서첩 시중 노승섭작가 발굴〉

From poverty and prosperity, all lie under heaven's hand;

Let fate unfold in its own time, and nature take command.

Wealth and glory seldom come to one arm in solitude;

Reputation, unclaimed, in turn travels without prelude.

When path calls for haste—then walk slow, be measured in your strides;

When climbing first—beware the fall that pride within provokes.

Brushing through this dusty world, along an uncertain road,

Even behind another's shadow, refrain from lashing your own load.

A Poem Written in Yi Sun-sin's Youth

A Poem from Admiral Yi Sun-sin's Memoir Booklet,

Discovered by Writer No Seung-seop

문인에서 무인으로
From Scholar to Warrior

이순신은 1565년 아산 백암리에 살던 방 씨와 혼인을 한다. 보성군수를 지낸 장인 방진의 후원으로 본격적으로 병학을 배우면서 28살이 되던 해 1572년(선조5년) 별과 시험에 응시한다. 어린 시절 군사놀이를 하며 놀았던 고향 남산 밑 훈련원에서 무과 시험을 보던 중 말에서 낙마하여 다리가 부러지는 사고를 당한다. 주변 사람들 모두가 기절했다고 생각했으나, 정신을 가다듬고 일어나 옆에 있던 버드나무 껍질을 벗겨 다리를 동여매고 끝까지 시험을 치른다. 아쉽게도 시험에서는 낙방하였지만 포기하지 않는 끈기와 집념을 보여준다. 〈출처-이충무공전서〉

이순신은 실패를 두려워하지 않았으며 한번 세운 목표는 어려움이 있더라도 끝까지 밀고 가는 사람이었다. 그리하여 4년 뒤인 1576년(선조 9년) 그의 나이 32살에 식년시 무과에 급제하여 관직에 오른다.

훈련원은 이순신 장군의 생가터와 그리 멀지 않은 곳에 위치해 있었다. 병사들의 무술 훈련과 병서, 전투대형등의 강습을 맡았던 곳이다. 조선 태조 원년(1392년)에 설치되어 여러 명칭으로 바뀌다가, 태종 때 지금의 자리(서울 중구 을지로 227)로 옮겨 짓고, 청사 남쪽에 활쏘기 등 무예를 연습하고 무과 시험을 보는 대청인 사청을 지었다. 이렇게 5백여 년 이상의 역사를 갖고 조선의 여러 가지 군사 관련 업무를 진행하였던 곳이다. 지금은 훈련원도 역사와 시간의 흐름 속에 본래의 모습은 사라지고 재정비되어, 훈련원공원이란 이름으로 도시인들의 휴식터로 변모되었다.

In 1565, Yi Sun-sin wed Lady Bang of Baekam-ri in Asan. Through the support of his father-in-law, Bang Jin, once magistrate of Boseong, he immersed himself more deeply in the study of military arts. By 1572, at the age of twenty-eight, he stood for the state military examination. The venue was the Hullyeonwon*, the Royal Military Training Center at the foot of Namsan, where he had once played at war as a boy.

Fate tested him harshly that day. Yi was thrown from his horse, his leg shattered. On-lookers believed him lost to unconsciousness. Yet he rose, steadied his breath, and tore the bark from a willow tree to bind his broken limb. With pain surging through him, he returned to the field and completed the exam. Though he did not pass, his endurance and unyielding will became evident to all. (Source: Complete Works of Admiral Yi Sun-sin)

Yi Sun-sin feared no failure. Once a goal was set, he pressed forward relentlessly, no matter the hardship. Four years later, in 1576, at the age of thirty-two, he succeeded in the national military examination and began his official career as a soldier of Joseon.

Hunryunwon Park The Formal Royal Military Training Center of the Joseon Dynasty

Located at 227 Eulji-ro, Jung-gu, Seoul, this park marks the historic site of the Hunryunwon, the military training ground of the Joseon Dynasty. Established in 1392 under King Taejo and renamed during King Sejo's reign in 1466, the Hunryunwon served as the center for martial arts practice, military drills, and state military examinations (Mukwa).

The original wooden structures, once built from red pines felled on Mount Baekdu and transported down the Amnok River, have since disappeared. However, timbers recovered during demolition were repurposed to craft a commemorative signboard, preserving the memory of the past.

훈련원 전경 *The Hunryunwon Training Ground*

시련과 단련 : 전쟁을 준비하다

Trials and Discipline – Preparing for War

무관이 되어
Becoming a Military Officer

32세에 무과에 급제했지만 보직을 얻지 못하다가, 1년 후 험한 산골 함경도 삼수 동구 비보로 부임하여 초급 장교로 근무하게 된다. 여진족의 침범에 대비해 군사훈련을 시키던 중 함경도 감사 이후백이 관할 장수들을 모아 활쏘기 시험을 시행한다. 뛰어난 활쏘기로 이순신은 명성을 날린다.

35세에 훈련원 봉사(종8품)로 승진하여 한양으로 와 인사를 담당하게 된다. 상관인 병조정랑 서익이 인사 청탁을 해왔으나, 특정인을 위하여 순서를 바꿀 수 없다며 완강하게 거부하며 대치한다. 훈련원 봉사로 8개월을 봉직하고, 같은 해 10월 충청 병사의 군관이 되어 충청도 해미로 간다. 충청도 해미에서 9개월을 머물다가

36세 1580년 만호(종4품)로 승진하여 전라남도 고흥군 도화면에 있는 발포로 간다. 직속상관인 성박이 거문고를 만들려고 오동나무를 베어오라고 발포로 사람을 보내자 "이것은 나라의 물건이라 개인 용도로 쓸 수 없다. 또 심은 사람의 뜻이 있을 터인데 어찌 오래된 고목을 베어 국용에 쓰지 않고 사사로운 물건을 만든단 말이냐?"며 심부름꾼을 나무라며 돌려보낸다. 이같이 이순신은 올곧고 불의에 타협하지 않는 성품이었다. 이런 탓에 발포 만호로 지내며 훈련원 인사 담당을 했을 당시, 청탁을 거절당한 서익이 군시경차관으로 나와 군기를 제대로 보수하지 않았다며, 앙심을 품고 상부에 거짓 보고하여 발포 만호 18개월 만에 처음 파직을 당한다.

38세 1582년 1월, 4개월 만에 만호(종4품)에서 봉사(종8품)로 하향 조정되어 훈련원으로 복직한다. 강직하고 청렴한 성품의 이순신은 파직 당시, 어렸을 때 이웃(서울 묵정동)에 살았던 류성룡이 이순신의 친척인 율곡 이조판서를 찾아가 보라고 권하나 "집안 친척이니 찾아봄직도 하지만 인사권을 가지고 있을 때 찾아가는 것은 옳지 않다."며 거절한다.

39세 발포에서 인연이 있었던 이용이 함경도 남병사로 가게 되면서, 이순신을 자신의 군관으로 삼겠다며 조정에 특청을 넣어 다시 함경도로 가게 된다. 같은 해 10월 이순신은 조선의 최북단인 경원고을 건원보로 옮겨간다. 어느날 여진족이 침략해 와서 학익진과 같은 전술을 펼쳐 여진족을 모두 소탕하는 쾌거를 이룬다. 다음 달 아버지가 향년 73세로 세상을 떠나셨다는 부음을 받고 이슬을 밟고 출발하여 별이 뜰 때까지, 한번도 쉬지 않고 천리길을 말을 타고 달려가 상복을 입자, 주변 사람들이 감탄을 했다고 한다.

42세에 삼년상을 마치고 복사 주부(종6품)가 되어 한 달간 수레와 말과 목축 일을 맡다가, 다시 여진족의 침략을 막기 위해 만호(종4품)로 승진하여 함경도 경흥고을 조선보로 간다.

43세 1587년 8월 조선보와 20리 거리에 있는 두만강이 바다로 들어가는 어귀에 있는, 녹둔도 둔전관을 겸임하게 된다.

At the age of thirty-two, Yi Sun-sin passed the Military Service Examination, yet no post was granted to him. A year later, he was dispatched to Donggubi Fort in the rugged mountains of Samsu, Hamgyeong Province, to serve as a junior officer. There, while preparing his men against raids by the Jurchens, the provincial governor, Yi Hu-baek, held an archery contest among his commanders. Yi's remarkable skill with the bow quickly won him renown.

At thirty-five, he was promoted to Bongsa (a junior official, 8th rank) at the Hul-lyeonwon in Hanyang, where he oversaw military appointments. When his superior, Seo Ik of the Ministry of War, sought to manipulate appointments for personal gain, Yi firmly refused, declaring that he would not alter the order of promotion for anyone. After serving eight months in this post, he was reassigned in October as a staff officer to the provincial commander in Chungcheong, stationed at Haemi. He remained there for nine months.

At thirty-six, in 1580, he was elevated to Manho (a defense commander, 4th rank) and posted to Balpo in Goheung County, Jeolla Province. His superior, Seong Bak, ordered him to cut down a paulownia tree to make a geomungo (a zither). Yi rebuked the messenger, saying, "This is the property of the state and not for private use. Moreover, the man who planted it left his intent in the roots. How can we cut such an old tree to fashion a personal instrument, instead of preserving it for public need?" His incorruptible nature left him vulnerable. Seo Ik, still bearing a grudge from his earlier refusal, falsely reported that Yi had neglected military upkeep. Thus, after only eighteen months as commander of Balpo, Yi was dismissed from office for the first time.

At thirty-eight, in January 1582, after only four months, he was reinstated at the Hul-lyeonwon, but at the lower rank of Bongsa. Known for his integrity and uprightness, Yi was advised by his childhood neighbor, Ryu Seong-ryong, to seek out his distant kinsman, Yi I (Yulgok), then Minister of Personnel. Yi declined, replying, "Though he is kin, it is improper to approach him while he holds authority over appointments."

At thirty-nine, Yi's old acquaintance, Yi Yong, became Commander of Southern Hamgyeong and petitioned the court to have Yi appointed as his officer. That October, Yi was sent to Geonwon Fort in Gyeongwon, the northernmost frontier of Joseon. When the Jurchens launched an attack, Yi employed tactics akin to the crane-wing formation (Hakikjin), utterly routing the invaders. Soon after, he received word of his father's death at the age of seventy-three. Mounting his horse, he rode tirelessly through the night and day, over a thousand li, until the stars faded, arriving in mourning clothes at his father's bier—a display of filial devotion that moved all who witnessed it.

At forty-two, after three years of mourning, Yi was appointed Boksa Jubu (6th rank) and briefly managed logistics of wagons, horses, and livestock. Soon, he was again promoted to Manho to defend Joseonbo Fortress in Gyeongheung, Hamgyeong Province, against renewed Jurchen incursions.

At forty-three, in August 1587, he also assumed charge of Nokdun-do, a fortified granary at the mouth of the Tumen River where it flows into the sea, about twenty ri* from Joseonbo.

* **Ri (리)** A traditional Korean unit of distance, roughly 400 meters (0.25 miles).

첫번째 백의종군
The First 'Baekui-jonggun'

녹둔도는 고원지대에서는 군량미를 생산해 내는 유일한 곳이었다. 1587년 9월 1일 경흥부사 이경록과 함께 군대를 인솔하여 녹둔도로 가서 추수를 하는 사이, 추도에 살고 있던 여진족이 사전에 화살과 병기류를 숨겨 놓고 있다가 기습 침입하여 녹둔도 전투가 벌어진다. 녹둔도 전투에서 조선군 11명이 죽고 160여 명이 잡혀갔으며 15필의 말을 약탈당한다. 이순신의 상관인 북병사 이일은 도망치고 이순신과 이경록은 끝까지 싸워, 그 결과 승리했으며 조선인 백성 60여 명을 구출한다.

이 전투로 책임을 지게 된 복병사 이일은 이순신에게 그 죄를 덮어씌우고 이경록과 이순신을 수감하고, 적호가 녹둔도의 목책을 포위했을 때 군기를 그르쳤다며 조정에 장계를 올린다. 이경록과 이순신을 모함하고 있다는 사실을 눈치챈 선조는 한 번의 실수로 사형은 과하다며 북병사 이일에게 장형을 집행하게 한 다음, 백의종군 시키라고 지시하여 위기에서 벗어난다.

이후 이순신은 북병사 휘하에서 백의종군*하며 1588년 2차 녹둔도 정벌에서 여진족 장수 우을기내를 잡은 공으로 사면을 받아 복직하게 된다.

*백의종군 (白衣從軍) 백의종군은 조선시대에 사용된 형벌로 관직 없이 군대를 따라 전장에 참여하는 것을 의미한다. 직무 권한은 박탈당하지만, 전직 관료 신분으로 현직을 보좌하는 처분을 뜻한다. 장군의 옷은 붉고 색이 화려하나 일반 백성의 옷은 하얗듯이 흰옷을 입고 장군이 아닌 백성으로서 군대에서 일을 하는 것에서 유래한다.

Nokdun-do, a frontier granary on the high plains, was the only place in the region that could yield military provisions. On September 1, 1587, Yi led troops there alongside Yi Gyeong-rok, the magistrate of Gyeongheung, to oversee the harvest. Yet the Jurchens of Chudo, who had hidden weapons and arrows in advance, launched a sudden ambush, sparking the Battle of Nokdun-do*. In the fighting, eleven Joseon soldiers were slain, more than 160 were captured, and fifteen horses seized. Yi's superior, Yi Il, the Northern Provincial Commander, fled the field. Yi Sun-sin and Yi Gyeong-rok fought to the end, and though bloodied, they prevailed—rescuing over sixty of their countrymen.

But disgrace sought them in victory. Yi Il, held responsible for the debacle, shifted the blame onto Yi Sun-sin and Yi Gyeong-rok, accusing them of disorder in command when the Jurchens encircled the palisade at Nokdun-do. He sent a memorial to the court denouncing them. King Seonjo, discerning the falsehood, judged that execution for a single failure was too severe. Instead, he ordered Yi Il himself punished with flogging, while commanding that Yi Sun-sin serve in Baekui Jonggun*—'in the ranks in white robes.' Thus did Yi escape death, but not disgrace.

Yi continued under the Northern Commander in this humbled role, following the army without office or command. In 1588, during the second campaign against Nokdun-do, Yi distinguished himself by capturing the Jurchen leader Ulginae. For this, he was pardoned and restored to his rank.

*The Battle of Nokdun-do (1587)
At Nokdun-do, Admiral Yi Sun-sin and Governor Yi Gyeong-rok repelled a Jurchen raid, rescuing civilians despite heavy losses. Wrongly blamed by his superior, Yi was demoted to Baekui Jonggun ('service in white robes'), which only reinforced his image of loyalty and resilience.

*Baekui-Jonggun (白衣從軍)
A Joseon disciplinary measure where dismissed officials served the army as commoners. The term reflects the contrast between generals' crimson robes and the plain white of the people, symbolizing a fallen officer stripped of rank yet still contributing.

이순신의 사람들
The Men Beside Admiral Yi

인사가 만사라고 하듯, 훌륭한 사람 곁에는 훌륭한 사람들이 있다. 이순신 장군이 많은 해전을 치루며 큰 업적을 남긴 데에는 몸을 아끼지 않고 조국을 위해 헌신한 사람들이 있다. 이들의 충심과 업적을 헤아려 본다. 〈출처-이순신의 파워인맥 제장명저〉

01. 정운, 조선수군 최고의 돌격장이 되다
02. 권준, 이순신의 마음을 읽다
03. 어영담, 물길의 달인으로 조일전쟁을 승리로 이끌다
04. 이순신(李純信), 한산도해전에서 일본군을 유인하여 승리에 기여하다
05. 배흥립, 이순신과 함께 수군 재건의 핵심 활동을 하다
06. 김완, 이순신의 휘하로 칠천량해전까지도 참전하다
07. 나대용, 조선 최고의 전투선인 거북선을 설계하다
08. 이봉수, 화약 제조의 1인자가 되다
09. 이언량, 거북선의 돌격장이 되어 전투를 승리로 이끌다
10. 정사준, 정철총통으로 화포의 효율성을 높이다
11. 유형, 이순신의 후계자로 우뚝 서다
12. 송희립, 현장 전술의 귀재로 노량해전의 승리에 기여하다
13. 송여종, 한산도 진중 과거 급제자로 절이도해전의 일등 공신이 되다
14. 정경달, 이순신의 대변인으로 종횡무진하다
15. 안위, 이순신과 함께 명량해전을 승리로 이끌다

As the saying goes, "Personnel is everything." Great leaders are never alone; beside every great commander stand men of equal loyalty and resolve. Admiral Yi Sun-sin's unmatched record in countless battles was not his alone—it was sustained by those who gave their strength, their skill, and even their lives for the nation. Here, we honor the devotion and deeds of those who fought at his side. (Source: Yi Sun-sin's Network of Power, Je Jang-myeong)

1. Jeong Woon – Became the most formidable assault captain of the Joseon navy.

2. Gwon Jun – Read the heart of Yi Sun-sin with keen insight.

3. Eo Yeong-dam – A master of waterways who guided Joseon to victory.

4. Yi Sun-sin (李純信) – Lured and turned the tide at Hansando.

5. Bae Heung-rip – Worked at Yi's side to rebuild the navy from ruins.

6. Kim Wan – Followed Yi even into the disastrous Battle of Chilcheollyang.

7. Na Dae-yong – Designed the Turtle Ship, Joseon's greatest war vessel.

8. Yi Bong-su – Rose as the foremost expert in gunpowder production.

9. Yi Eon-ryang – Led the Turtle Ship in charges that brought victory.

10. Jeong Sa-jun – Improved firepower efficiency with the Jeongcheol cannon.

11. Yu Hyeong – Stood tall as Yi Sun-sin's successor.

12. Song Hee-rip – A tactical genius who helped secure victory at Noryang.

13. Song Yeo-jong – Passed the military exam and rose as a hero at Jeoleido.

14. Jeong Gyeong-dal – Served as Yi's spokesman, swift and tireless.

15. An Wi – Fought alongside Yi to win the Battle of Myeongnyang.

16. Je Man-chun – Supplied Yi with critical intelligence on enemy movements.

17. Yi Ui-on – Secured military provisions through the naval pass system.

18. Choi Hui-ryang – Took charge of rebuilding the navy's core strength.

19. Jeong Dae-su – Showed Joseon's fighting spirit to Ming generals.

20. Bae Gyeong-nam – A model of devotion in his care for the navy.

21. Yi Yeong-nam – Became Yi's close aide even while serving under Won Gyun.

22. Ma Ha-su – Led evacuation vessels that brought victory at Myeongnyang.

23. Yi Hu-baek – Instilled in Yi the upright bearing of a true official.

24. Jeong Eon-sin – Recommended Yi and became his genuine teacher.

25. Yu Seong-ryong – Yi's lifelong mentor, who nominated him as Commander

26. Yi Won-ik – Reported Yi's achievements with accuracy and fairness.

27. Jeong Tak – Saved Yi Sun-sin's life through steadfast loyalty.

28. Jeong Geol – Passed down thirty years of battlefield experience to Yi.

29. Won Gyun – Rival and reluctant ally, both clashing with and aiding Yi.

30. Go Sang-an – Fellow candidate, founder of the naval exam.

31. Seon Geo-i – A comrade met on the battlefield, who shared in hard-won victories.

32. Yi Eok-gi – Joined forces with Yi to form a united fleet.

33. Chen Lin (Jin Lin, 陳璘) – Admiral of Ming China, fought with him at Noryang.

이순신의 사람들
The Men Beside Admiral Yi

거북선
The Construction of the Geobukseon

거북선은 임진왜란에서 활약했던 조선 수군의 군함이다. 세계 최초의 완전 밀폐 전투를 상정한 화약시대 함선이다. 왜적은 당시 조선의 주력 무기인 활보다 유효 거리가 두 배 가까이 되고, 총알의 속도와 파괴력도 활보다 훨씬 빠른 조총으로 무장했다. 이순신은 해전이 일어날 것을 예측하고, 왜적을 이기기 위해서는 조총을 이길 새로운 무기가 필요하다고 생각했다. 이러한 필요성에 의해 거북선이 건조된다.

때마침 판옥선을 설계하던 나대용이 그리고 있던 전선을 말아서 전라 좌수사로 부임해 온 이순신을 찾아간다. 왜군의 조총에 맞서기 위해 신무기가 필요하다고 생각했던 이순신은 조정에 장계를 올리고 조선 기술을 겸비한 걸출한 나대용과 대목수 한 대선 등 여러 전문 인력을 동원한다. 이순신 장군의 지도 아래 전통을 바탕에 두고 과학적인 연구와 새로운 구상을 덧붙여 그리고, 세우고, 부수고를 반복하며 군과 민이 하나가 되어 왜적에 맞서 싸울 거북선을 건조한다. 임진왜란이 터지기 하루 전날, 드디어 1년 만에 목을 길게 뺀 거북선이 등에 쇠촉을 세우고 위엄 당당한 모습으로 탄생한다.

애국심이 빚은 조선 최고의 창조적인 산물!
거북선은 기적을 만들어가며 전공을 세우는데 큰 활약을 한다.

The Geobukseon*, Turtle Ship was the war vessel that distinguished itself in the battles of the Imjin War. It was the world's first fully enclosed combat ship, conceived in the gunpowder age. At the time, the Japanese were armed with arquebuses—matchlock muskets whose range was nearly twice that of the Korean bow, and whose speed and destructive force surpassed arrows by far. Foreseeing that future battles at sea would pit musket against bow, Admiral Yi Sun-sin realized that Joseon needed an entirely new weapon if it was to prevail. From this necessity, the Turtle Ship was born.

At that time, Na Dae-yong, who had been sketching plans for the Panokseon (Joseon's multi-decked warship), sought out Yi, newly appointed as Commander of the Left Naval District of Jeolla. Yi, equally convinced of the need for a new weapon against the Japanese muskets, submitted a memorial to the court and rallied the finest minds of Joseon: Na Dae-yong, master shipwright Han Dae-seon, and other skilled craftsmen. Under Yi's direction, drawing upon tradition while daring new designs, they sketched, built, dismantled, and rebuilt. Soldiers and civilians alike labored as one, until at last the vessel took form. On the eve of the Imjin War, after a year of relentless effort, the Turtle Ship emerged—its long neck crowned with a dragon's head, its back armored with iron spikes—an awe-inspiring creation ready for battle.

It was a product of patriotism, Joseon's most ingenious invention, and it would soon carve miracles upon the seas, securing glory in battle.

*Geobukseon Turtle Ship

거북선의 특징적인 제원
Distinctive Features of the Turtle Ship

조선의 선박 형태인 판옥선을 기본 선체로 하고 복층 구조로 하여 아래층에서는 노를 젓고 위층에서는 포와 활을 쏘는 전투 행위를 한다. (승선 인원 약 150명)

Built upon the hull of the Panokseon, with a two-deck structure: rowers beneath, gunners and archers above (crew of about 150).

앞은 용머리 형태이며 입을 통해 대포를 쏜다.

The prow shaped like a dragon's head, from whose mouth cannons could be fired.

뒤는 거북이 꼬리 형태이며 밑에 총구멍이 있다.

The stern fashioned like a turtle's tail, with gunports beneath.

등은 거북이 등처럼 판자로 덮고 그 위에 촘촘히 쇠못을 박아, 왜군이 배에 올라오지 못하도록 막는 역할을 한다.

The deck covered like a turtle's shell, studded with iron spikes to prevent enemy boarding.

좌우에는 6개씩 총포 구멍이 있다.

Six gunports on either side.

안에서는 밖을 내다볼 수 있으나 밖에서는 안을 볼 수 없다.

The interior allowed vision outward, while shielding those within from outside view.

각종 총통 등 모든 무기를 사용할 수 있다.

Equipped to fire a wide array of cannons and weapons.

강한 재질인 조선 적송으로 만들어져 일본 전함에 비해 매우 견고하다.

Constructed of resilient red pine from Joseon, far sturdier than Japanese vessels.

포함 기능뿐 아니라 적선과 충돌하여 파괴하는 돌격선 기능도 가능하다.

Functioned both as a warship and as a ramming vessel, able to crush enemy ships in collision.

주요 부분은 철판으로 두른 철갑선이어서 적의 총탄과 화력을 막을 수 있다.

Parts of the hull reinforced with iron plating, making it resistant to bullets and artillery fire.

충심이 빚은 조선 최고의 창조적 산물이 건조되다

The Birth of Joseon's Greatest Creative Invention, Forged in Loyalty

신은 이미 준비를 마쳤나이다
I Am Already Prepared.

일은 미리 생각해 두면 이루어지고 미리 생각하지 않으면 망치게 된다. 말하기 전에 미리 생각해 두면 막힘없이 유창하고, 일하기 전에 미리 생각해 두면 일하기가 곤란하지 않으며, 실행하기 전에 미리 생각해 두면 후회하지 않게 되고, 인간의 도리를 실천하는 방법이 미리 준비되면 막히는 일이 없을 것이다 〈중용 20장〉

1592년 전라 좌수사 이순신은 임진왜란을 예측하고 이를 대비해 숨 가쁘게 토의하고, 보고하고, 조사하고, 궁리하는 등 해전을 위한 만반의 준비를 갖춘다. 관할 밖인 경상도 지역에 대한 정보도 수집하고, 동시에 부근 섬을 정찰하게 하고, 각 도의 물길을 살피고, 군사들이 모일 지점까지 전략과 전술에 필요한 모든 정보를 수집한다.

충분한 인적 물적 준비를 해 왔기 때문에, 20여 척이 조금 넘는 조선 수군은 500여 척이나 되는 적의 함대를 상대해 전쟁을 승리로 이끈다.

이순신은 정성스러운 사람이었고 유비무환* 정신은 그의 업적에 근간을 이루는 중요한 요소이다. 매사에 철저하게 준비한 뒤 앞으로 나아갔으므로 어려운 상황에 처해도 동요되지 않고 성공의 길로 나아갈 수 있었다.

"신은 이미 준비를 마쳤나이다."

*유비무환 (有備無患) '미리 준비하면 근심이 없다'는 사자성어로 중국의 고서 '서경'에서 유래한다

If one anticipates beforehand, the task will be accomplished; if not, it will be ruined.

If thought precedes speech, one speaks with clarity.

If thought precedes action, the work will not falter.

If thought precedes execution, one will have no regret.

If the way of human duty is prepared in advance, nothing will obstruct it.

— Doctrine of the Mean, Chapter 20

In 1592, as Commander of the Left Naval District of Jeolla, Yi Sun-sin foresaw the coming war with Japan. He set about with tireless urgency—deliberating, reporting, investigating, and devising—to ensure complete readiness for battle at sea. He gathered intelligence not only from his own district but also from Gyeongsang, beyond his jurisdiction. He dispatched scouts to nearby islands, charted the waterways of each province, and identified rallying points for his forces. Every detail required for strategy and tactics was examined and secured.

Thus, when war erupted, the Joseon fleet of barely more than twenty ships faced an enemy armada of over five hundred and prevailed. Victory was the harvest of foresight.

Yi Sun-sin was a man of meticulous devotion. The spirit of Yubimuhwan*—'with preparation, there will be no fear'—was the foundation of his success. He advanced only after every measure was readied; thus, even in dire peril, he did not waver but pressed forward on the path of triumph.

"I am already prepared."

*Yubimuhwan (有備無患)
Meaning "If one is prepared, one need not worry," originates from the ancient Chinese classic Book of Documents (Shujing).

물속에 담긴 글 *Letters Carried by the Sea*

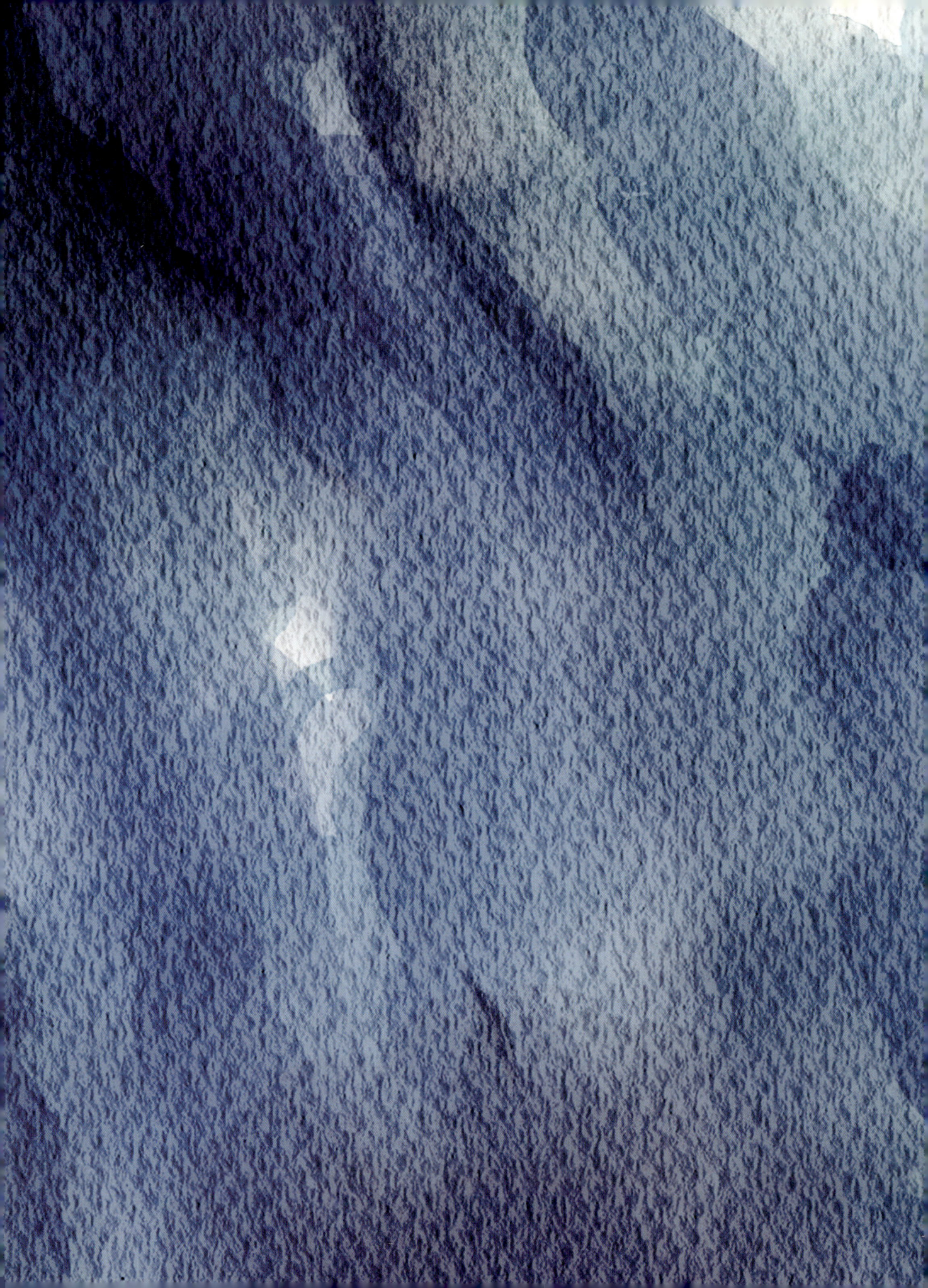

불멸의 전쟁사 : 승리의 기록

Immortal Chronicles of War – Records of Victory

옥포해전
The Battle of Okpo

"산처럼 묵직하고 침착하라."

1592년 5월 7일 임진왜란 발발 후 이순신이 첫 번째 해전을 치러 승리로 이끈 전투다. 옥포는 현재 거제도에 있는 포구이다.

조선의 영호남 함대는 50여 척의 왜전선들이 4월 27일부터 부산, 김해 등에서 살인, 방화 등 갖은 만행을 저지른 후, 5월 7일 옥포만에 도착해 있다는 걸 포착한다.

이순신은 대장선에 올라 첫 전쟁, 첫 출전이라 긴장되어 있는 장병들에게 "함부로 움직이지 말고, 산처럼 묵직하게 침착하라."며 전령을 외친다. 각종 총통화기를 퍼붓고 공격하여 옥포 해전을 승리로 이끈다. 그 후 옥포 인근 합포에서도 왜선 5척을 파괴하고 적진포 (현재 통영시 광도면 적덕동)에서도 왜선 11척을 불태우는 전과를 올린다.

이것이 이순신이 거둔 제1차 해전 옥포대첩이다.

"Steady as a Mountain, Calm as Stone."

On May 7, 1592, just days after the outbreak of the Imjin War, Admiral Yi Sun-sin led his men into their first battle—and their first victory. The battle took place at Okpo, a harbor on present-day Geoje Island.

The combined Joseon fleets of Yeongnam and Honam learned that some fifty Japanese warships had anchored at Okpo Bay. These ships had left Busan and Gimhae on April 27, committing atrocities of slaughter and arson as they advanced.

Yi Sun-sin mounted his flagship and addressed his men, tense and anxious for their first engagement. "Do not act rashly," he commanded. "Be steady, calm, and unmoving—as a mountain." At his signal, the Joseon navy unleashed volleys of cannon fire and pressed the attack. The enemy fleet was routed, and the Battle of Okpo ended in resounding victory.

Yi's forces then struck again, destroying five Japanese ships at Happo, and burning eleven more at Jeokjinpo (in present-day Gwangdo-myeon, Tongyeong).

Thus was won Admiral Yi's first triumph at sea: the Battle of Okpo.

사천해전
The Battle of Sacheon

거북선 출항하다

1년에 걸쳐 준비한 거북선은 임진왜란이 일어나기 하루 전에 완성되었으나, 첫 번째 해전인 옥포해전에서는 사용하지 않고, 두 번째 해전인 사천해전에서 첫 출항을 한다.

이순신이 제1차 옥포해전을 치르고 여수 본영으로 돌아와 다음 출전을 위해 장병 징집, 군선 정비 등을 하고 있을 때 왜선들은 점점 경상 해안 서쪽으로 침범해 온다. 이에 5월 29일 다시 출전하여, 사천선창(현재 용현면 선진)에 배들을 매어놓고 육지로 올라와 분탕질을 치고 있던 왜군들을 공격하고, 짐짓 패한 듯이 물러나자 왜군들이 쫓아오며 사천만 한가운데로 유인되어 나온다.

이때 이순신은 2척의 거북선을 앞세워 적선을 향해 돌진케 하였으며, 왜적도 조총을 난사하며 치열한 접전이 시작된다. 이순신은 제2차 해전인 이 전투에서도 대승을 거두었으나 안타깝게 어깨에 총탄을 맞는다. 어깨 부상으로 한동안 고생한 기록이 일기에 고스란히 적혀 있다.

사천해전은 처음으로 거북선이 출전하여 놀라운 활약을 한 의미 있는 전투이다.

The Turtle Ship Sets Sail for the First Time

After a year of preparation, the Turtle Ship was completed on the very eve of the Imjin War. Yet it was not employed in the first engagement at Okpo, but rather in the second great battle—at Sacheon.

Following the victory at Okpo, Yi Sun-sin returned to his base at Yeosu to rally his men and refit his fleet for the next campaign. Meanwhile, the Japanese pressed farther west along the Gyeongsang coast. On May 29, Yi again put to sea. At Sacheon, the enemy had moored their ships at the wharf of Seonchang (today's Seonjin, Yonghyeon-myeon) and were plundering inland.

Yi feigned retreat, luring the Japanese fleet into open waters at Sacheon Bay. Then, at his command, two Turtle Ships surged forward, charging headlong into the enemy. The Japanese responded with volleys of musket fire, and a fierce battle ensued. Yi's forces won a decisive victory, but he himself was struck in the shoulder by a bullet—a wound he later recorded with pain in his War Diary.

The Battle of Sacheon thus marked the Turtle Ship's first appearance, a moment of astonishment and significance in Joseon's naval history.

한산도대첩
The Great Victory at Hansando

통영 한산도 앞 바다, 포위 섬멸 전술인 학익진이 처음으로 펼쳐진 해전이다.

일본 수군 구성	와키자카 야스하루	70여 척
	구키 요시타카 및 가토 요시아키	40여 척
조선 수군 구성	이순신과 이억기	48척
	원균	7척

일본 함대는 견내량(현재: 거제시 사등면 덕호리)에 정박하고 조선 함대는 당포에 정박 집결하였다. 견내량은 거제도와 통영만 사이에 있는 긴 수로로 길이 4km에 폭은 600미터를 넘지 않고, 암초가 많아 조선의 판옥선이 운신하고 전투를 벌이기에는 좁은 해역이었다. 그런 반면에 한산도는 거제도와 통영 사이에 있어 사방으로 헤엄쳐 갈 길도 없고 무인도라 상륙해도 먹을 것이 없는 섬이었다. 이순신은 왜군을 넓은 바다로 유인하여 학이 날개를 펼치듯 감싸서 섬멸하는 전략을 세운다.

조선 수군 판옥선 5~6척이 적을 덮치듯이 진격하다 도망치자 일본 함대는 도망가는 조선 전선을 잡으려고 유인되어 몰려 내려왔다. 이때 섬들 뒤에 숨어있던 조선 전선들이 일제히 양쪽에서 학이 날개를 펴듯 왜군 함대를 감쌌다. 이순신 장군은 학익진 전법으로 일본 함선 59척을 격침 또는 나포하여 한산도에서 대승을 거둔다. 이때 조선 수군의 사상자는 있었으나 전선의 손실은 전혀 없었다.

한산도해전은 일본 수군의 주력을 거의 격파해 그들의 수륙병진 계획을 좌절시켰다. 그리고 육지에서 잇단 패전으로 사기가 떨어진 조선군에게 승리의 용기를 주었다. 또한 조선 수군이 남해안 일대의 제해권을 확보함으로써 이미 상륙한 적에게도 위협을 주어 불리하던 전세를 유리하게 전환할 수 있었다.

한산도해전은 조선군이 학익진 전법을 이용해 왜군을 크게 무찌른 해전이며 세계 해전 중에서도 손꼽히는 자랑스러운 해전에 속한다.

—

It was off the coast of Hansando, near Tongyeong, that Admiral Yi Sun-sin first employed the Hakikjin—the Crane-Wing Formation, a tactic of encirclement and annihilation.

Japanese Fleet	Wakisaka Yasuharu Kuki Yoshitaka & Kato Yoshiaki	Estimated 70 ships Estimated 40 ships
Joseon Fleet	Yi Sun-sin & Yi Eok-gi Won Gyun	48 ships 7 ships

The Japanese anchored at Gyeonnaeryang (today's Deokho-ri, Sadeung-myeon, Geoje), a narrow strait 4 km long and less than 600 meters wide, strewn with reefs—ill-suited for the maneuvering of Joseon's Panokseon warships. Hansando, by contrast, lay between Geoje and Tongyeong: an isolated island, with no food to forage and no escape by sea. Yi devised a strategy to lure the enemy into open waters and there envelop them, as a crane spreads its wings.

Five or six Panokseon slipped into the waters off Hansando, feigning retreat. The Japanese, eager to seize the fleeing ships, gave chase. Then, from behind the cover of islands, the hidden Joseon fleet emerged—closing in from both flanks, wings outstretched. The Japanese were encircled and crushed. Fifty-nine enemy ships were sunk or captured, while Joseon suffered casualties but lost not a single warship.

The victory at Hansando shattered the main strength of the Japanese navy, halting their plan to advance by land and sea in concert. For the Joseon army, demoralized by repeated defeats on land, it restored courage and resolve. By securing command of the southern seas, the navy threatened enemy forces already ashore and turned the tide of war in Joseon's favor.

The Battle of Hansando was not only a triumph of Admiral Yi's Crane-Wing Formation, but also one of the most brilliant naval engagements in world history.

The Battle of Hansando was not only a triumph of Admiral Yi's Crane-Wing Formation, but also one of the most brilliant naval engagements in world history. Like Themistocles at Salamis, who broke the Persian fleet upon the narrow straits, and like Nelson at Trafalgar, who shattered Napoleon's ambitions upon the seas, Yi Sun-sin at Hansando turned the tide of war through genius, discipline, and resolve.

This victory was more than a clash of ships; it was the vindication of foresight, preparation, and unity. The waters of Hansando bore witness to a moment when Joseon, against overwhelming odds, secured command of the sea. From that day, Admiral Yi's name would stand among the great captains of history, and Hansando would shine as a beacon in the annals of naval warfare.

한산도 대첩 *Battle of Hansando*

학익진
The Crane-Wing Formation

학익진은 진법의 일종으로 학이 날개를 펴는 모양을 본떠, 상대의 주변으로 원을 그려가면서 둘러싸고 화력을 집중 퍼부어 섬멸시키는 전술이다.

이순신 장군이 사용한 진법은 단순한 학익진보다 초승달 형태의 어린 학익진을 사용했는데, 이는 물고기의 비닐이 벌려진 것 같은 대형인 어린 진과 학이 날개를 편 모양과 같은 학익진이 결합된 전술이다.

학익진의 핵심은 화력의 집중인데 횡진을 짜고 화력을 일 점에 집중시켜 적의 선단을 격파하는 것이다. 방법적으로는 전군의 진형을 좌, 중, 우 셋으로 나누어 중군이 적의 주 공세를 받아내는 동안 상대적으로 압력을 적게 받는 좌, 우, 군이 측면을 공격하는 것이다. 이는 화력을 일 점에 집중하도록 만들어, 그 위력을 극대화할 뿐 아니라, 적이 방호하기 어려운 측면을 포함하여 전방위를 집중 공격함으로써 병력 피해와 사기 저하를 꾀하는 것이다. 학익진은 넓은 횡대 진형이므로 각 부분들끼리 서로 멀어지고 진형의 중심이 얇아지는 상황이 전개되므로, 전군을 통제하고 적시에 전술 행동을 시킬 수 있도록 많은 훈련이 필요하다.

이순신은 평소에 병사들의 숙련도를 정예화하고 자원적, 시간적 여유와 지형적 조건들을 분석하여 이 전술을 사용하였다. 조선군의 화포가 가진 우수한 사거리와 화력, 판옥선의 선회 능력과 요새 수준의 견고함, 그리고 자신이 길러낸 조선 수군의 단합력을 최대한 이용하였다. 학익진 전법은 한산도대첩만이 아니라 이후의 해전에서도 사용되어 전쟁을 승리로 이끌었다고 전해진다.

The Hakikjin, or Crane-Wing Formation, was a tactical array modeled on the wings of a crane in flight. The fleet would spread outward in a wide arc, encircling the enemy and pouring concentrated firepower into the trapped formation until it was annihilated.

Yet Admiral Yi Sun-sin did not employ the simple Hakikjin alone. Instead, he devised a hybrid—a crescent-shaped formation resembling the scales of a fish, combined with the outward sweep of a crane's wings. This adaptation allowed him to harness both encirclement and concentrated fire in unison.

The essence of the Crane-Wing tactic was concentration. The fleet, drawn up in three divisions—left, center, and right—would engage so that the center bore the enemy's assault while the wings struck from the flanks. By focusing all fire upon a single point, Yi's fleet shattered the enemy line, while simultaneous attacks from the sides overwhelmed their defenses, inflicting heavy casualties and breaking their morale.

Such a tactic demanded discipline. The wide span of the formation left its center thin, and coordination across the fleet required precise timing and constant training. Without rigorous preparation, the array would collapse upon itself.

Yi Sun-sin ensured its success by forging his men into an elite force, drilling them to mastery, and calculating every factor—resources, time, terrain. He exploited the strengths of Joseon arms: the superior range and power of its cannons, the maneuverability and fortress-like resilience of the Panokseon, and above all the unity he had instilled in his sailors. The Crane-Wing Formation, first unveiled in the great victory at Hansando, would be employed again in later battles, carrying Joseon to triumph upon the waves.

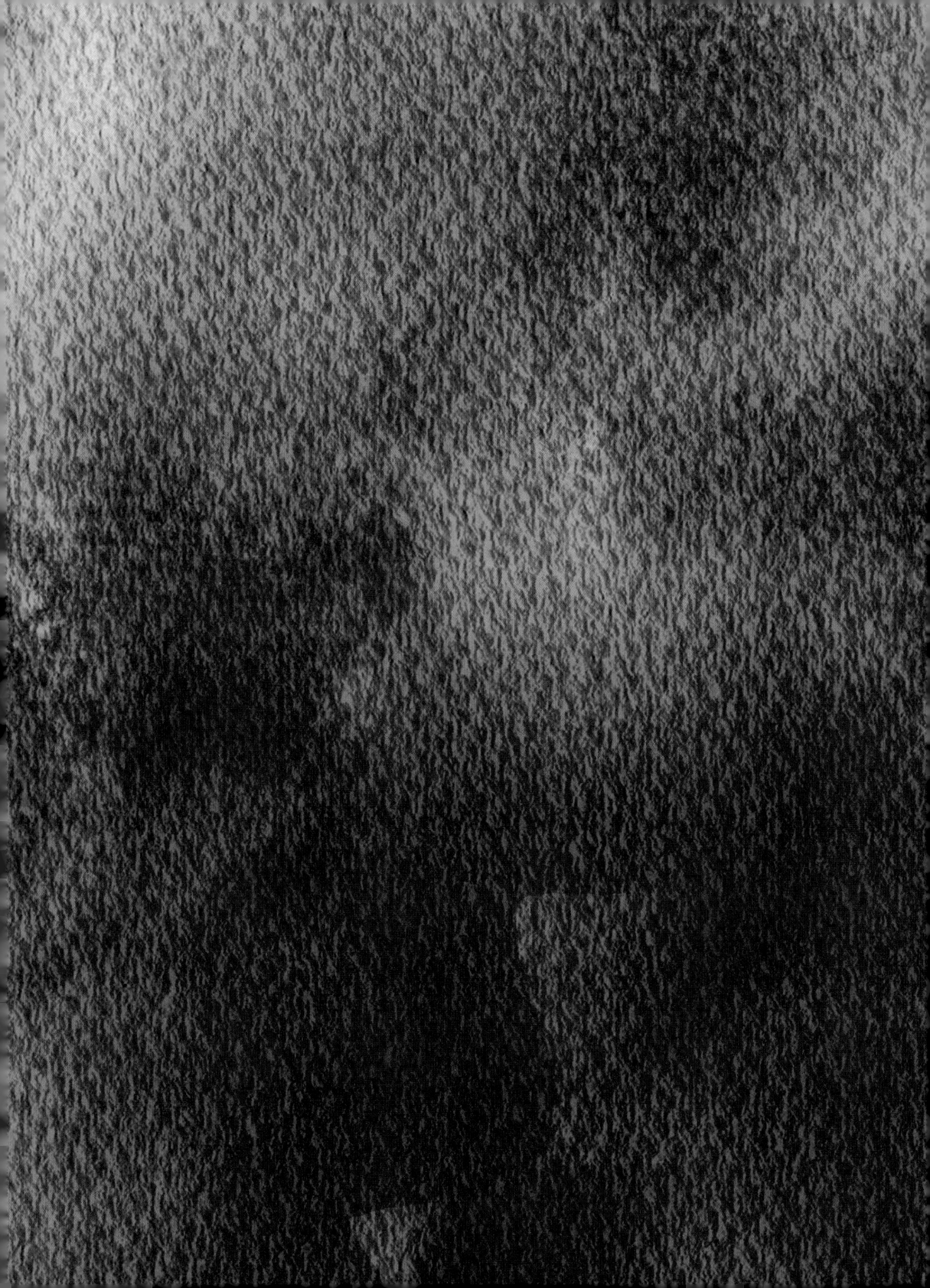

인간 이순신 : 고뇌와 상실

The Man Yi Sun-sin – Anguish and Loss

부하 장수의 죽음을 애도하며
Mourning the Deaths of His Officers

이순신은 부하 장수들에게도 예를 다하는 사람이었다. 장수들의 지식과 의견을 존중하였으며 몇 차례 해전을 치르는 동안 여러 부하 장수, 군사들을 잃으며 애통해하고, 잠을 이루지 못하며 가슴을 쓸어내리곤 하였다. 신분 고하를 막론하고 전사자들에게는 예를 갖춰 장사를 지내주고, 그들의 공을 세세히 적어 상부에 보고하고 가족들을 구휼 하였다. 다음은 아끼던 부하 장수 정운*을 잃고 쓴 글이다.

어허, 인생이란 반드시 죽음이 있고
죽고 삶에는 반드시 천명이 있나니
사람으로서 한번 죽는 것은 진실로 아까울 게 없건마는
오직 그대 죽음에는 마음 아픈 까닭이 있다
나라가 불행하여 섬 오랑캐 쳐들어와
영남의 여러 성이 바람 앞에 무너지자
몰아치는 그들 앞에 어디고 거침없어
우리 서울 하루 저녁 적의 소굴 이루도다
천리 관서로 님의 수레 옮기시고
북쪽하늘 바라보면 간담이 찢기건만
슬프다 둔한 재주 적을 칠 길 없을 적에
그대 함께 논의하자 해를 보듯 밝았도다
계획을 세우고서 배를 이어 나갈 적에

죽음을 무릅쓰고 앞장서 나가더니

왜적들 수백 명이 한꺼번에 피 흘리며

검은 연기 근심 구름 동쪽 하늘 덮었도다

네 번이나 이긴 싸움 그 누구 공로런고

종사를 회복함도 기약할만 하옵더니

어찌 뜻했으랴 하늘이 돕지 않아 적탄에 맞을 줄을

저 푸른 하늘이여 알지 못할 일이로다

돌아올 제 다시 싸워 원수 갚자 맹세터니

날은 어둡고 바람조차 고르잖아 소원을 못 이루매

평생에 통분함이 이 위에 더할쏘냐

여기까지 쓰고 나도 살을 에듯 아프구나

믿는 이 그대인데 인제는 어이할꼬

진중의 모든 장수 원통히도 여기거니와

그 재주 다 못펴고 덕은 높되 지위 낮고

나라는 불행하고 군사 백성 복이 없고

그대 같은 충의는 고금에 드물거니

나라 위해 던진 그 몸 죽어도 살았도다

슬프다 이 세상에 누가 내 속 알아주리

극진한 정성으로 한잔 술을 바치노라

어허, 슬프도다

*녹도만호 충장공 정운 (1543년~1592년)

정운은 전라남도 영암 출신으로 이순신보다 2살 많고 무과도 6년이나 앞서 급제한 사람이다. 이순신의 충실한 부하 장수로서 이순신 장군과 함께 부산포 해전에 참전하여 대승을 거두었으나 안타깝게도 적탄에 맞아 전사하였다. 이순신은 정운 장군을 무척 신뢰하였으며 이순신이 보낸 장계에서 '녹도만호 정운은 맡은 바 직책에 충실하고 담략까지 겸비하여 신이 어려운 일을 같이 의논할 수 있었던 사람이었습니다' 라고 평하였다. 정운 장군은 아끼던 보검에 검명을 '정충보국'이라 새겼다. 이 뜻은 '올곧은 충심으로 나라에 보답한다'라는 의미이니 장군의 높은 충심을 읽을 수 있다.

Admiral Yi Sun-sin was a leader who treated even his subordinates with the utmost respect. He valued their knowledge and counsel, and through the many battles he fought, he grieved deeply for those he lost. Sleepless nights and heavy sighs marked the passing of his fellow commanders and soldiers. Regardless of rank or station, he ensured proper burials for the fallen, recorded their deeds in detail for the court, and cared for their families.

On the right page appears a lament he composed upon the death of his beloved subordinate, Jeong Woon*.

Ah! Life must end in death,
And death and life are both decreed by Heaven.
To die once as a man is no cause for regret—
Yet your passing rends my heart with sorrow.

The nation was in peril, the island invaders swarming,
The fortresses of Yeongnam toppled like grass before the wind;
They pressed forward without hindrance,
Until even Seoul lay at risk in a single night.

Northward, your bier is borne a thousand li,
And gazing upon the sky, my very soul is torn.
When no means remained to smite the foe,
You stood beside me, bright as the rising sun.

In planning our course, in lining up the ships,
You faced death head-on, leading from the front.
Hundreds of foes fell at once in blood and smoke,
Dark clouds of grief veiled the eastern sky.

Four victories we counted—whose merit but yours?

Even the hope of restoring our realm could be pledged on you.

Yet Heaven withheld its favor, and shot you down with enemy fire;

Ah, blue sky above, inscrutable your ways!

You swore to return, to avenge the foe once more,

But night fell, the winds turned ill, and fate denied your wish.

What greater grief could this life contain?

Even as I write, the pain cuts my flesh.

You were my truest companion—what shall I do now?

All in camp lament with bitter hearts.

Your talents unspent, your virtue great, your rank too low,

Our nation unblessed, our soldiers and people bereft.

Such loyalty and righteousness—rare through all ages;

For the country you gave your life, and thus you live still.

Alas! Who in this world will know the depth of my heart?

With utmost devotion, I offer you this cup of wine.

Ah, how bitter my grief!

*Jeong Woon (1543~1592)
Commander of Nokdo, posthumously honored with the title 'Lord of Loyal Valor (忠壯公)'

Jeong Woon, Chungjanggong, commander of Nokdo (Manho), hailed from Yeongam, Jeolla Province. Two years senior to Yi Sun-sin and successful in the military examinations six years earlier, he fought faithfully under Yi's command. Together they won a great victory at the Battle of Busan, but Jeong fell to enemy fire. Yi praised him in an official memorial: "Commander Jeong Woon of Nokdo fulfilled his duties with diligence, combining loyalty with tactical acumen. He was a man with whom I could consult on the gravest of matters." Jeong engraved upon his treasured sword the words 'Jeongchung Boguk' ("With upright loyalty, I repay my country"), a testament to his indomitable spirit of fidelity.

부하 장수의 죽음을 애도하며 *Elegy for a Loyal Commander*

한산도 생활
Life on Hansando

1593년 전쟁이 명과 왜의 강화 협상하에 소강상태로 접어들고, 이순신은 삼도수군통제사라는 직책으로 충청, 전라, 경상 3도의 수군을 총괄하는 수장으로 한산도에 주둔하게 된다. 왜군이 남쪽 경상도 연해안으로 철수하여 12개의 성을 쌓고 장기전으로 돌입하니, 이를 견제하며 강화 협상이 결렬되는 정유년 (1597년)까지 약 4년 동안 한산도에서 머무르게 된다.

이순신의 한산도 생활의 목표는 왜선이 서쪽으로 진입하려면 거쳐야 하는 견내량을 지키는 일과, 종국적으로 전쟁의 재발에 대비해 철저한 준비를 해두는 것이었다. 1595년 7월 1일 난중일기에 그의 우국충정을 읽을 대목이 있다.

'홀로 다락 위에 기대어 나라 돌아가는 꼴을 생각하니 위태롭기가 아침 이슬과 같다. 안으로는 정책을 결정할 만한 기둥 같은 인재가 없고 밖으로는 나라를 바로 잡을 주춧돌 같은 인물이 없으니, 모르겠다 나라의 운명이 어떻게 되어갈지… 마음이 괴롭고 종일 엎치락 뒤치락했다' 〈출처-난중일기, 노승석 저〉

이순신의 한산도 생활은 심적으로 힘든, 쓸쓸하고 고독한 시간이었다. 몇 차례 전쟁을 치른 후이고 또 다음 해전에 대비해야 하나 병졸들은 굶주림과 전염병으로 고생하니, 이를 보는 이순신의 걱정과 고민은 깊어만 갔다. 줄어든 군사, 빈약한 전력, 나날이 불어나는 왜적 선단, 이런 상황에서 서해로 나가는 가장 요긴한 길목을 오직 제힘으로 혼자 책임지고 지켜내야만 했기 때문이다. 하지만 어려운 상황에서도 스스로 재원을 만들어 인적 물적 전력을 증강하였으며, 적에 관한 정보수집에도 심혈을 기울였다.

그러던 중 원균이 이순신의 심기를 불편하게 만들고 결국은 각종 모함으로 이순신은 투옥되는 상태에 이른다. 외딴 척박한 남쪽 섬에서 오직 국가만을 위해 봉직하며 4여 년 동안 잠 못 이루며 보낸 장군의 쓸쓸함이 여러 시에서 나타난다. 〈출처-이충무공전서〉

한산도가

한산섬 달 밝은 밤에

수루에 홀로 앉아

큰 칼 옆에 차고

깊은 시름하는 차에

어디서 일성호가는

남의 애를 끊나니

한산도의 밤

한바다에 가을빛 저물었는데

찬바람에 놀란 기러기 높이 떴구나

가을에 근심 가득 잠 못 이룬 밤

새벽 달 창에 들어 칼을 비추네

무제

가을 기운이 바다에 들어오니 나그네 회포가 어지럽다

홀로 봉창 아래 앉으니 마음이 몹시도 번거롭네

달빛은 뱃전에 비치고 정신도 맑아져서

잠을 이루지 못하는 새에 어느새 닭이 운다

In 1593, as peace negotiations unfolded between Ming and Japan, the war entered a lull. Yi Sun-sin was appointed Samdosuguntongjesa—Commander of the Combined Fleets of the Three Provinces of Chungcheong, Jeolla, and Gyeongsang—and stationed at Hansando. The Japanese, withdrawing to the southern coast of Gyeongsang, built twelve fortresses and prepared for a protracted war. Yi remained at Hansando for nearly four years, until negotiations collapsed and hostilities resumed in 1597.

Yi's foremost task was to defend Gyeonnaeryang, the narrow strait through which the Japanese would have to pass if they attempted to push westward. At the same time, he prepared meticulously for the inevitable renewal of war. His War Diary entry of July 1, 1595, reveals his anguish:

"Alone I leaned against the railing of the watchtower, pondering the fate of the nation, fragile as morning dew. Within, there is no pillar strong enough to guide policy; without, no cornerstone to uphold the state. I know not where our destiny lies… My heart is heavy, and I toss and turn all night long." (Nanjung Ilgi, annotated by Noh Seung-seok)

Life at Hansando was one of solitude and hardship. Though he had already fought several battles, he could not rest, for the enemy still loomed. His soldiers, weakened by hunger and disease, weighed heavily upon his mind. With diminished forces and poor supplies, he bore alone the burden of guarding the most vital passage to the West Sea, even as the enemy fleet grew daily in strength. Yet despite the adversity, Yi managed to raise his own resources, strengthen both men and arms, and devote himself to gathering intelligence on the foe.

Amid these struggles, rivalries with Won Gyun led to slanders that eventually saw Yi imprisoned. On this remote and barren island, for more than four sleepless years, he served his nation in loneliness. His sorrow and devotion echo in the poems he left behind. (Source: Collected Works of Admiral Yi Sun-sin)

Hansando

On Hansan Isle, beneath the moon's bright glow,

Alone I sit upon the tower's height;

My great sword rests beside me as I brood,

Deep sorrow fills my heart this silent night.

From somewhere comes the call of a lone crane,

Its cry tears at my soul with grief unspoken.

A Night on Hansando

Across the sea, autumn light fades to dusk,

Wild geese, startled by the chill wind, rise aloft.

Through autumn nights, laden with restless care,

The dawn moon enters my window, glinting on my sword.

No Title

Autumn's breath sweeps in across the sea,

And stirs the wanderer's heart with restless longing.

Alone beneath the eaves I sit in disquiet,

Moonlight gleams on the prow, my spirit made clear.

Yet sleepless, I wait, until at last the cock crows.

투옥
Imprisonment

이순신의 한산도 생활 막바지인 정유년(1597년)을 전후로 그를 몰락시키고자 하는 음모가 두 곳에서 생겨난다.

첫 번째 음모는 이순신을 제거하고 자신이 통제사가 되기 위해 온갖 수단을 동원해 온 원균과 그와 뜻이 통했던 이 일, 그리고 윤두수 등 일부 서인 세력의 음모였다.

그들은 군졸들을 굶기면서 군량미를 횡령하여 그것으로 뇌물 삼아 한양의 대신과 비빈, 내시들과 연계하여 이순신을 모함했다. 이들은 이순신은 싸움을 기피한다, 원균이 세운 전공을 가로챈다, 자신에게 잘못이 있으면 이를 감추고 왕에게는 허위를 보고한다 등의 헛소문을 퍼트렸다. 이에 편향된 성격을 지닌 선조는 이를 진실인 양 받아들였다. 이순신의 운명은 조정 대신들의 무책임한 말에 따라 점점 수난의 길로 빠져들었다.

두 번째는 왜적의 이순신 제거 음모다. 일본 장수 고니시가 간첩 가나메 도키스라를 내세워 조선 조정을 흔드는 이간 정책을 세운다. 가나메는 어리석은 경상우 병사 김경서를 이용해 조선 조정에 많은 허위 정보를 제공해 온 사람이었다. 가나메는 김경서에게 일본 장수 가토가 일본에서 조선으로 바다를 건너올 건데, 이때 통제사가 수군을 이끌고 가서 처치할 수 있다는 정보를 흘린다. 김경서는 이를 권율을 통해 즉시 조정에 보고하고 이에 임금은 출전을 명령한다. 하지만 이순신은 전쟁 상식으로 간첩의 말은 믿을 게 아니라며 여러 날 동안 출전하지 않는다. 나랏말을 받들지 않았다는 이유로 결국 이순신은 체포되어 한산섬 생활 3년 8개월 만에 한양으로 압송된다. 이순신이 한산섬을 떠나는 1597년 2월 26일 온 섬이 남녀노소 할 것 없이 수많은 백성들의 곡성으로 젖었다.

옥중에 갇힌 이순신은 심한 고문을 당하며 죽음에 직면한다. "죽고 사는 것은 천명이니 죽게 되면 죽을 것이다." 뇌물을 쓰면 나갈 수 있다는 말에도, 죽음에 직면해서도, 남을 원망하거나 타락함을 갖지 않는 성정이었다.

하지만 정박 등 기타 뜻 있는 선비들과 몇몇 중신의 간언이 주효해 선조가 마음을 바꾸고 결국 이순신은 사형 직전까지 갔다가 백의종군하라는 명령을 받고 옥문을 나온다.

—

Toward the end of Yi Sun-sin's years at Hansando, around 1597, two conspiracies arose to bring about his downfall.

The first was plotted by Won Gyun, who sought to remove Yi and claim the post of Tongjesa (Commander of the Three Provinces) for himself. He found allies in Yi Il and Yun Du-su, along with other Western faction officials. They starved the soldiers, embezzled military provisions, and used them as bribes to court eunuchs, consorts, and ministers in Hanyang, spreading slanders against Yi. They accused him of shirking battle, stealing credit for Won Gyun's victories, concealing his own mistakes, and deceiving the king with false reports. King Seonjo, quick to suspicion, accepted these calumnies as truth. Yi Sun-sin's fate grew ever darker, bound by the careless words of men at court.

The second plot came from the enemy itself. Konishi Yukinaga, the Japanese commander, dispatched the spy Kaname Tokisura to sow division in the Joseon court. Kaname had long manipulated Gyeongsang's provincial commander Kim Gyeong-seo, feeding him false intelligence. He now spread word that the Japanese general Katō Kiyomasa would soon cross from Japan, and that the Tongjesa could intercept him if he sallied forth. Kim relayed this to General Gwon Yul, who in turn pressed the king. Seonjo commanded Yi Sun-sin to sortie. But Yi, knowing the stratagem of spies, refused to act on such words. For several days he held his fleet in port. His refusal to obey what he deemed folly was seized upon as defiance of the royal command. Thus, after three years and eight months on Hansando, Yi was arrested and sent in chains to Hanyang.

On February 26, 1597, as Yi departed Hansando, the island was drowned in lamentation. Men and women, young and old, wept openly; the air itself seemed steeped in sorrow.

It was more than grief—it was testimony. The cries of the people were not only for the departure of a commander, but for the injustice of a nation that had condemned its truest guardian. Their lament was the voice of conscience, proclaiming what the court would not: that Admiral Yi Sun-sin's honor was beyond slander, and that his fidelity was the people's shield. In their wailing was both sorrow and defiance, for even stripped of title and bound in chains, Yi remained the nation's hope.

In prison, Yi endured severe torture and stood at the threshold of death. Yet he remained steadfast: "Life and death are in Heaven's hands; if I am to die, then so be it." Though told that bribes could purchase freedom, he refused corruption, never yielding to bitterness or despair.

At last, thanks to the pleas of upright scholars such as Jeong Bak and the intercession of several loyal ministers, King Seonjo relented. Yi Sun-sin, brought to the very brink of execution, was spared—only to be stripped of rank and condemned to serve once more in Baekui Jonggun ('in the ranks in white robes'). He walked free of the prison gates, his honor stained, yet his spirit unbroken.

어머니의 죽음
The Death of His Mother

이순신의 어머니는 초계변씨 수림의 딸로 1515년 생이다. 친정은 충남 아산 고을 백암리 지방의 유지였으며 유복한 가정이었다. 어머니는 자식들을 사랑을 다해 키우면서도 가치를 중시하였다. 시집 형편이 어려워지자 이순신이 10~12살(추정) 때 모든 가솔을 이끌고 아산 친정 동네로 이사할 만큼 담대한 성품이었다. 아산으로 온 뒤로는 친정의 도움과 그 스스로 각고의 노력으로 많은 가산을 모아, 남편이 죽은 후 자식들에게 재산을 골고루 나누어 주었다. 어머니 나이 78세인 1592년 난리가 나자, 이순신은 가족들을 여수 본영에서 가까운 부하 장수 정철의 집을 빌려(여수 쌍봉 응천리 곰내 마을) 피난시켰다. 곧 다른 가족들은 아산 본가로 돌아가고 어머니 혼자만 계속 여수에 머무르게 된다. 어머니가 혼자 여수에 머문 이유는 이순신이 어머니를 곁에 두고 모시기 위함이라고도 하고, 자식을 가까이서 돌봐야 한다는 어머니의 강한 의지일 수도 있다고 전해진다. 이순신은 어머니를 '천지' 즉 하늘이란 뜻으로 호칭하며 존경하였다.

"어머니를 모시고 함께 한 살을 더하게 되니 이는 난리 중에도 다행한 일이다." 이와 같이 그의 일기에는 어머니에 대한 이야기가 자주 나온다. 어머니께 문안한 일, 소식을 듣는 일, 음식을 보내는 일, 걱정하는 일, 지극 정성으로 효도한 일 등이 소상히 적혀 있다. 이순신이 어려울 때마다 내리는 간결한 결단력의 근원지가 바로 어머니였고, 담대한 성정과 충만한 사랑의 성품 또한 그 어머니로부터 연유되었다.

1597년 정유년 어머니는 이순신이 누명을 쓰고 압송되자, 자식의 뒤를 돌보려고 고령의 나이에 죽음을 무릅쓰고 1,000리 뱃길로 나선다. 여수를 떠나 거친 서해를 항해하다 향년 83세로 영면에 드셨다. 이때 이순신은 옥에서 풀려난 지 10일째였으며 시신을 모신 배가 해암 바닷가로 들어오자 이순신은 배 위로 올라가 통곡하며 울었다.

> 충성을 다하려 했더니 죄가 이미 이르렀고
> 효성을 바치려 했건만 어버이 마저 가 버렸네
> 이제 어서 죽기만 기다려야 할런가
> 마을을 돌아보니 가슴은 찢어지고
> 비조차 내리는데 금오랑*은 길 재촉하네
> 천지에 나 같은 사람 또 어디메 있을꼬

*금오랑
신라 화랑 전통과 삼족오(태양의 상징) 에서 비롯된 고사적, 상징적 표현. 이순신 장군의 시에서는 '시간을 재촉하는 존재, 인생의 무상함을 일깨우는 상징' 으로 쓰였다고 볼 수 있음.

Yi Sun-sin's mother was Lady Byun of the Chogye clan, Surim's daughter, born in 1515. Her family, local gentry of Baekam-ri in Asan, Chungcheong Province, was prosperous and respected. She raised her children with steadfast love and instilled in them the values of integrity and honor. When her husband's household fell on hard times, she displayed great resolve, leading the entire family back to her natal home in Asan when Yi was about ten to twelve years old.

There, aided by her kin and through her own tireless effort, she restored the family's fortunes. After her husband's death, she distributed property fairly among her children.

In 1592, when war erupted, she was seventy-eight. Yi arranged for his family to take refuge at the home of his subordinate Jeong Cheol in Gomnae Village, near Yeosu. Soon, the others returned to their ancestral home in Asan, but Lady Byun remained in Yeosu. Some say Yi kept her close to serve her, others that she herself insisted on staying near her son in troubled times. Yi referred to his mother as Cheonji—'Heaven and Earth'—a title of reverence.

Yi's War Diary is filled with entries about his mother: asking after her health, sending food, worrying over her well-being, expressing gratitude for her presence. He regarded the gift of sharing another year with her, even in wartime, as a blessing. His clarity in decision and his indomitable spirit were rooted in her courage and love.

In 1597, after Yi was disgraced and taken in chains to Hanyang, Lady Byun, then eighty-three, resolved to follow him. Braving a thousand li across the rough West Sea, she perished during the voyage. Yi, newly released from prison, learned of her passing ten days later. When the boat carrying her body arrived at the shore of Haeam, he climbed aboard and wept aloud in anguish.

At last, thanks to the pleas of upright scholars such as Jeong Bak and the intercession of several loyal ministers, King Seonjo relented. Yi Sun-sin, brought to the very brink of execution, was spared—only to be stripped of rank and condemned to serve once more in Baekui Jonggun ('in the ranks in white robes'). He walked free of the prison gates, his honor stained, yet his spirit unbroken.

I strove for loyalty, yet guilt was laid upon me;

I longed to show my filial heart, yet my parent is gone.

Now must I only wait in silence for death?

As I look upon the village, my heart is torn apart.

Rain falls, while Geumo-rang* urges me on my way.

Where in all Heaven and Earth is there one so bereft as I?

*Geumo-rang
Meaning 'Sun Crow Youth,' a symbolic figure associated with the three-legged crow in the sun, representing the fleeting passage of time.

곡 (哭)
Longing for My Mother

절망 속의 희망 : 재기의 길

Hope Amid Despair – The Road to Redeption

신에게는 12척의 전선이 있습니다
I Still Have Twelve Warships Left

　1593년 계사년 진주성 전투 이후 왜군은 부산 등에 전진 기지만 확보 해 놓고 일본으로 철수했으며 명나라 군사도 본국으로 돌아갔다. 그 후 4년여에 걸쳐 명나라와 왜군 사이에 강화 교섭을 벌였으나 1596년 교섭은 결렬되고 왜군은 다시 조선을 침략하니, 이것이 1597년에 발발한 정유재란이다.

　이 사이 한산도에서 삼도수군통제사로 근무 중이던 이순신은, 원균 등 간신배들과 왜군 첩자 모략에 휘말려 투옥된 후 겨우 풀려나 도원수 권율 휘하로 백의종군하게 된다. 정유재란이 발발하고 왜군은 물밀듯이 바다와 육지로 침략해 수많은 백성을 죽이고 국토를 유린했다. 삼도수군통제사를 맡고 있던 원균은 안골포전투, 부산포전투에서 패하고 칠전량에서 조선 전선과 많은 군사들의 희생을 앞세우며 조선 해군사에 치욕적인 패배 기록을 남긴 채, 칠전량전투를 끝으로 53세 나이로 생을 마감한다.

　이 전투로 조선의 걸출한 수군 지휘관이 모두 사라지고, 이순신이 4년 동안 이루어 놓은 한산 진의 장엄한 모습은 한 줌 재로 변해버리고, 수년간 훈련한 정예병 수천 명이 전사하고, 피땀 흘려 건조한 거북선과 170여 척의 전함, 전투 장비들까지 일시에 물거품이 되고 말았다. 원균의 패전과 함께 삼도수군은 하루아침에 무너지고, 조선의 바다는 전함 한 척 없이 갈매기들만 바람을 타고 다녔다.

　도원수 권율 장군 휘하에 백의종군하고 있던 이순신은 권율의 허락 아래 패전으로 폐허가 된 해안가 여러 지역과, 흩어진 군사 전함들을 돌아보며 응전 대책과 구국의 방안을 생각하였다. 이때 한양의 조정은 왜적의 재침과 원균의 패전 소식을 듣고 크게 놀라며 대책을 강구하는 등 허둥지둥 흔들리다가, 대신 김명원, 이항복 등이 왜군들에게서 해상을 지킬 사람은 이순신 장군밖에 없다는 주청을 받고, 다급해진 선조는 별도리 없이 1597년 8월 3일 이순신을 다시 삼도수군통제사로 임명하게 된다.

다시 통제사가 된 이순신은 스스로 구국의 대책을 마련할 수 밖에 없었다. 자력으로 새로운 요충지를 구축하고, 군사를 불러 모으고, 부서지지 않는 배들을 모았다. 이때 모은 전함은 12척에 일반 백성들이 나중에 가져온 한 척이 더해져서 13척이 되었다. 무너져 버린 수군을 재건하여 왜군의 대선단을 대적하기에는 한참 열세하여 이순신은 진도 벽파진으로 진을 옮기고 전략과 전술을 준비한다. 조정에서는 이순신에게 빈약한 전선과 패잔병들을 데리고 의지할 곳 없이 해상을 떠돌 것이 아니라, 배를 버리고 육지로 올라와 적을 막으라고 명령한다. 수군 자체를 폐지하겠다는 뜻이었다.

이에 이순신은
"아직도 신에게는 12척의 전선이 있습니다."
"전선이야 비록 적지만
신이 죽지 않았으니 적이 감히 우리를 업신여기지 못할 것입니다."

보이는 것이 전부가 아니라는,
없는 것이 없는 것이 아니라는 의지를 보인다.

After the Battle of Jinju in 1593, the Japanese withdrew to their bases at Busan and other coastal fortresses, while the Ming forces returned to their homeland. For more than four years, negotiations dragged on between Ming and Japan. In 1596, talks collapsed, and the following year the Japanese launched their second great invasion of Joseon—the Jeongyu War.

During this time, Yi Sun-sin, still at Hansando as Tongjesa (Commander of the Three Provinces), fell victim to the intrigues of Won Gyun, corrupt courtiers, and Japanese spies. Stripped of command and imprisoned, he was released only to serve in Baekui Jonggun under General Gwon Yul, following the army without rank. When the war erupted in 1597, the Japanese surged across land and sea, slaughtering countless civilians and ravaging the land.

Won Gyun, who had been given Yi's command, led the navy into disaster. Defeated at Angolpo and Busanpo, he pushed the fleet into Chilcheollyang. There, he perished at the age of fifty-three, leaving behind one of the darkest stains in Joseon's naval history. The magnificent Hansan base that Yi had built over four years was reduced to ashes. Thousands of elite sailors trained through years of hardship were slain, the Turtle Ships and more than 170 war vessels destroyed. The navy of the Three Provinces collapsed in a single night, and the seas of Joseon lay barren, haunted only by gulls riding the wind.

As a humbled soldier under Gwon Yul, Yi walked the devastated shores, gazing upon the wreckage of ships and scattered soldiers. Grief weighed heavy, yet his mind turned ceaselessly to strategies of defense and salvation. In Hanyang, news of the Japanese return and Won Gyun's ruin threw the court into panic. Flustered and divided, ministers debated until Kim Myeong-won and Yi Hang-bok declared that none but Yi Sun-sin could restore command of the seas. Pressed by urgency, King Seonjo had no choice but to reinstate Yi as Tongjesa on August 3, 1597.

Yi, returned to command, could rely on nothing but himself. He rebuilt what he could, gathering men and salvaging the few ships that remained. Twelve warships were mustered, and later a thirteenth brought forth by commoners. Though outnumbered beyond measure, Yi shifted his base to Byeokpajin in Jindo, preparing strategies and tactics for the decisive clash to come. The court, despairing, ordered him to abandon the fleet and fight on land, effectively disbanding the navy.

Yi replied with words that would echo through the ages:

"Your servant still has twelve ships."
"Though our numbers are few,
while I yet live the enemy will never hold us in contempt."

In that declaration lay a truth beyond appearance: that what is seen is not all that is, and that even in seeming emptiness there may dwell an unyielding strength.

필사즉생 필생즉사
To Die Is to Live, To Live Is to Die

1597년 정유재란 칠전량해전 후 다시 삼도수군통제사로 임명된 이순신이 원균의 칠전량해전 패배로 괴멸된 조선 수군을 재건하기 위하여 흩어진 군사, 전함들을 모으며 진도 벽파진에 새로운 요충지를 구축하고 군사들을 재정비한다. 이를 눈치챈 왜적이 조선 수군을 말살시키기 위해 400여 척의 선단으로 대공세를 펼치려 하자, 이순신은 운명의 일전을 치러야 하는 시간이 다가옴을 직감한다. 전력의 막대한 차이를 극복하기 위해서는, 지형적 이점과 특별한 전술을 펼치지 않고는 불가능하다고 판단한다.

최후의 전투 장소를 명량(울둘목)으로 정하고 배수진을 친 후 명량해전을 앞두고 여러 장수를 불러 놓고 준엄한 훈시를 한다.

필사즉생 필생즉사
必死卽生 必生卽死

"반드시 죽으려고 하면 살 것이고
반드시 살려고 하면 죽을 것이다."

In 1597, after the disastrous defeat at Chilcheollyang, Yi Sun-sin was reinstated as Tongjesa (Commander of the Three Provinces). With the navy in ruins, he began to gather the scattered soldiers and ships, establishing a new stronghold at Byeokpajin in Jindo and painstakingly rebuilding his forces.

Sensing this, the Japanese prepared to annihilate him, assembling an armada of over four hundred ships. Yi, facing this moment of destiny, understood that only by exploiting the terrain and devising extraordinary tactics could he overcome such overwhelming odds.

He chose Myeongnyang (Uldolmok) as the place of battle, the narrow strait where the tides raged like a living force, and there he drew his baesujin—the 'do-or-die battle line.' On the eve of combat, he summoned his commanders and delivered words of iron resolve:

"He who is resolved to die shall live;
He who seeks only to live shall die."

These words, carved like iron into the hearts of his men, transformed despair into determination. With but a handful of ships, they would face an ocean of enemies—not clinging to life, but ready to stake all upon the fate of their country.

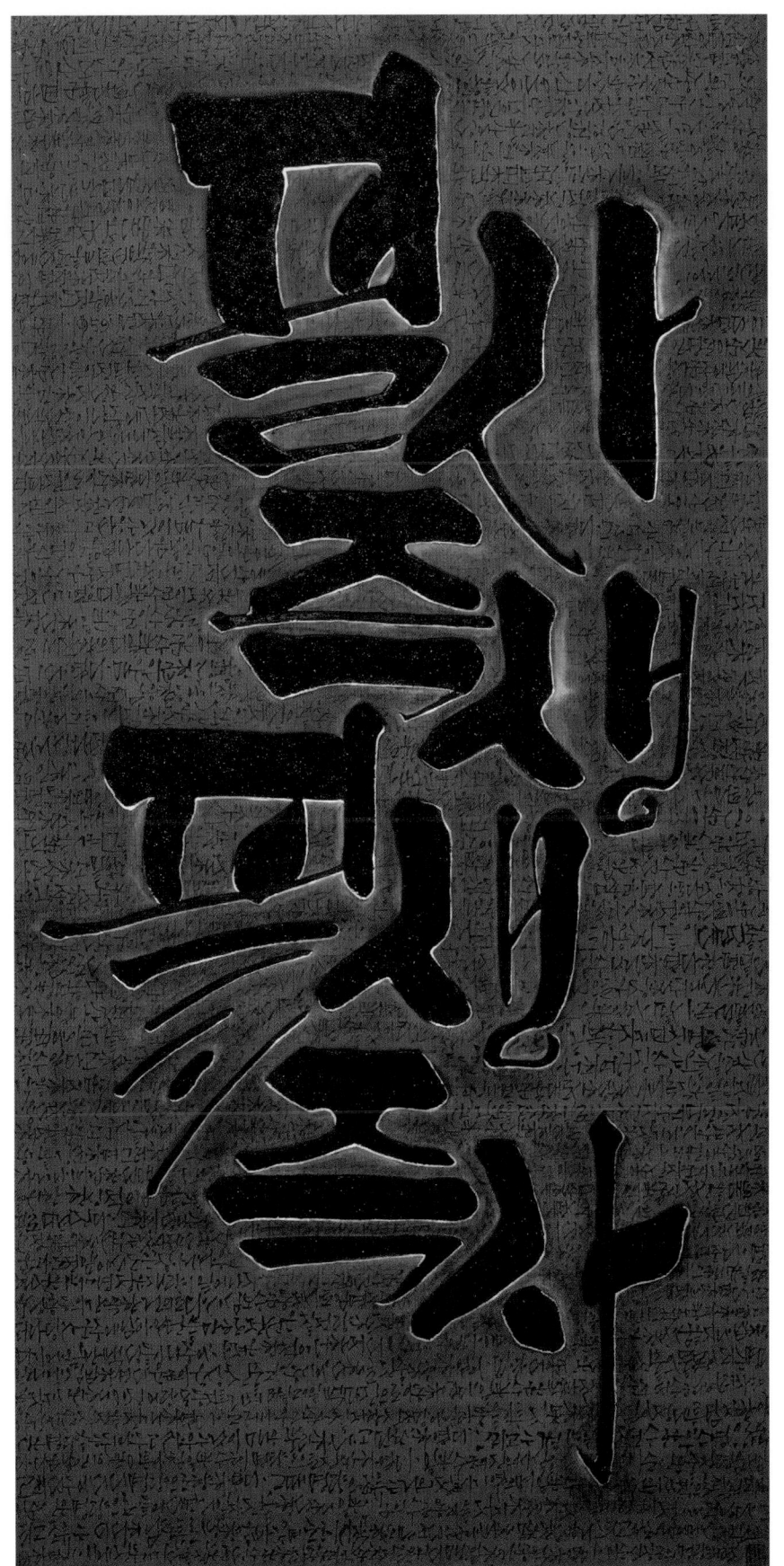

모래로 쓴 글 *To Seek Death Is To Find Life*

명량해전
The Battle of Myeongnyang

　1597년 이순신은 삼도수군통제사로 군사력을 정비하나 군중에 남아 있던 쓸만한 전선은 13척에 불과했다. 이때 일본 수군은 한산섬을 지나 남해안 일대로 침범하며 육군의 육상 진출에 맞추어 서해로 진출하려 하였고, 이순신은 이를 저지하기 위해 진지를 이진, 어린포 등지를 거쳐 8월 29일 벽파진(전라남도 진도군 고군면 벽파리)으로 이동했다. 일본 수군은 이곳을 여러 차례 기습하였으나 조선 수군의 강경한 방어로 패퇴하였다. 이후 명량을 등 위에 두고 싸우는 것이 매우 불리하다고 판단한 이순신은 진지를 우수영(전라남도 해남군 우수군 문내면)으로 옮긴다.

　우리 군사의 전함은 불과 13척인데 적의 군함은 무려 400여 척에 이르니 열세한 조건을 극복하기 위해서는 특별한 지형적 이점을 이용해야겠다고 생각하다가, 고심 끝에 선택한 장소가 명량이다. 명량은 전라남도 해남군 문내면 학동리에 있는 해협이며 별칭은 울둘목이라 불린다. 울둘목은 조수의 흐름이 빠르게 바뀌는 곳이다. 바닷목이 좁고 물살은 무척 세고 조수의 흐름이 폭포 같은 특이한 지역이라서, 이곳을 택하면 적이 많은 전함을 갖고 있어도 해협목으로 들어올 적함은 100여 척 정도를 넘지 못할 것이라 예상한다. 아군은 그들만 상대로 싸우면 되므로 전함의 열세를 최대한으로 줄일 수 있는 곳이라 생각한다.

　마침내 1597년 9월 16일 동서고금에 유래를 찾을 수 없는 역사적인 해전이 벌어진다. 이른 아침 133여 척의 일본 수군이 명량으로 진입한다. 이때 명량의 조류는 정조 시기였다. 조선 수군은 일자진을 형성하여 전투에 임하기로 하였으나 다른 전선들이 겁을 먹고 움직이지 않아, 혼자서 일본 수군 수십 척과 혼전을 벌이며 불사신 같은 기적을 만들어낸다. 일본 수군이 이순신이 타고 있던 전선을 포위 공격해 옴에, 이순신은 초요기를 올리고 뒤에 있던 거제현령 안위와 중군 김응함 등에게 적진으로 돌진할 것을 엄하게 명령한다. 이들에 이어 다른 전선들이 합류하며 전투는 절정에 이른다. 이때 조류는 서서히 남동류로 바뀌어 흐르고 수가 적은 조선 수군에 비해 많은 전선을 거느린 왜군에게 불리하게 덮쳐 진형과 대오를 무너뜨리기 시작한다. 또한 이순신 전선에 동승했던 투항왜인 준사가 일본 수군 장수 구루시마를 발견하고 외치자 본보기로 그를 끌어 올려 목을 베어 높이 매달자, 일본 수군의 사기는 극도로 저하되고 이에 전투의 기세를 잡은 조선 수군은 총통과 화전을 쏘며 맹렬히 공격하니 일본 수군은 패퇴하며 도주하고 만다.

13척의 배로 133척 이상의 배를 무찌른 명량해전은 세계 해전사 기록에 남을 대기록이다. 명량해전에서 조선의 전함은 단 한 척도 파손되지 않고 전체 사상자 수도 많지 않았으나 왜적의 전함과 인명피해는 막대하였다. 조선 수군을 위해 자연이 함께 싸워 준 해전이었다.

이 날의 승전으로 조선 수군은 재건의 기회를 잡았으며 잠시 잃었던 남해의 제해권을 탈환하고 왜의 서해 진출을 차단함으로써 조선군은 정유재란의 대세를 유리하게 전개할 수 있었다.

In 1597, reinstated as Tongjesa after the disaster at Chilcheollyang, Yi Sun-sin rebuilt what remained of the navy. Only thirteen warships could be mustered. The Japanese, meanwhile, advanced past Hansando and pressed along the southern coast, preparing to thrust into the West Sea to support their land campaigns. Yi shifted his base from Ijin and Eorinpo, eventually establishing a new stronghold at Byeokpajin in Jindo. Though attacked repeatedly, his fleet repelled the assaults. Judging Byeokpajin and even Yeosu vulnerable, Yi chose instead to move his fleet to Usuyeong, near present-day Haenam.

Against four hundred Japanese ships, Yi had but thirteen. To overcome such disparity, he determined to harness the terrain itself. His chosen ground was Myeongnyang Strait—also called Uldolmok, 'the Roaring Channel'—a narrow passage in Haenam where tides surged like waterfalls. Here, he reasoned, the enemy's vast numbers would be useless, for at most a hundred could press through at once, while his smaller force could concentrate their strength.

On September 16, 1597, one of history's most extraordinary naval battles began. At dawn, 133 Japanese warships surged into Myeongnyang. The tide was slack at first, and Yi formed his fleet in a line of battle. Yet fear gripped his captains, and none advanced. Alone, Yi led his flagship into the enemy, fighting dozens of ships in desperate combat, conjuring miracles from the edge of annihilation. The Japanese surrounded him, pressing hard, until Yi raised the command flag, summoning An Wi, magistrate of Geoje, and Kim Eung-ham, his center commander, to break into the fray. Their ships surged forward, followed at last by the others.

At that moment, the tide shifted, sweeping south-eastward. What had been a wall of Japanese ships was torn apart by the raging current. Their formations shattered, their lines broken, while the smaller Joseon fleet held firm in the torrent. Amid the clash, a surrendered Japanese, Jun-sa, sighted the enemy commander Kurushima. He cried out, and Kurushima was seized, beheaded, and his head raised high upon the mast—a sight that crushed Japanese morale.

Joseon cannons thundered; fire arrows rained. The Japanese fleet collapsed in panic, retreating in disorder. Yi's fleet, thirteen against more than a hundred, had triumphed. Not a single Joseon ship was lost, and casualties were few, while the enemy suffered ruin.

This was the miracle of Myeongnyang—a battle where nature itself fought for Joseon. The tide became an ally, the sea a weapon. With this victory, the navy seized its chance of rebirth, reclaimed command of the southern seas, and barred Japan's advance into the West. The war's course turned once more in Joseon's favor.

In the annals of world naval warfare, the Battle of Myeongnyang stands among the most astonishing feats of command. Like Themistocles at Salamis, who crushed a far greater Persian fleet in the narrow straits of Greece, or Nelson at Trafalgar, who secured Britain's mastery of the seas against Napoleon, Yi Sun-sin at Myeongnyang defied impossible odds with only thirteen ships. Yet unlike those battles, where forces were at least comparable, Myeongnyang was fought against a disparity so vast that its outcome seems miraculous. Historians across the world regard it not merely as a victory of arms, but as a triumph of leadership, discipline, and the will of a people who refused to surrender their seas.

통곡 : 면의 죽음
Lamentations : The Death of Myeon

이순신은 부인 방 씨 사이에 회, 열, 면 3형제와 딸 하나를 두었다. (일부 기록에는 회, 열, 면, 완 4형제를 두었다는 설도 있다) 회와 열은 이순신 휘하에서 일하였고 셋째 아들 면은 아산집에 남아 어머니를 모시고 있었다.

하루는 이순신이 꿈을 꾸었는데 아들을 데리고 말을 타다 말이 발을 헛디뎌 냇가로 떨어졌다. 거꾸러지는 막내 아들 면을 붙들어 안는 중에 꿈에서 깨었다. 아산에서 심부름꾼이 서신을 들고 와 봉투를 뜯어보니 아들 필체로 '통곡'이라는 글자가 쓰여있었다. 직감으로 면이 전사했다는 사실을 알아차렸다.

명량해전에서 참패한 적들이 아산 고을을 찾아가 이순신의 본가는 물론이고 온 마을에 불을 지르자, 어머니를 모시고 고향집에 있던 막내아들 면이 분함을 참지 못하고 적군 속으로 달려들어 싸우다가 21살의 나이로 순국한다. 대범하고 총명하여 장래 자신의 뒤를 이을 것이라고 기대를 해 온 자식이었기에 그 비통함은 이루 말할수 없었으리라. 심정을 이순신은 일기에 이렇게 적었다.

"간담이 떨어져 목을 놓고 통곡했다. 하늘이 어찌 이다지도 박정한고, 간담이 타고 찢어지는 것만 같다. 내가 죽고 네가 살아야 이치에 마땅한데, 네가 죽고 내가 살았으니, 이렇게 어긋난 일이 어디 있단 말이냐. 천지가 캄캄하고 해조차도 빛이 변했구나."

Yi Sun-sin and his wife, Lady Bang, had three sons—Hoe, Yeol, and Myeon—and one daughter. (Some records suggest a fourth son, Wan.) The elder sons Hoe and Yeol served under their father, while the youngest, Myeon, remained in Asan to care for his grandmother.

One night Yi dreamed that he was riding with his son, when the horse stumbled at a stream and both were thrown down. As he reached out to grasp his falling youngest child, he awoke. Soon after, a messenger from Asan arrived with a letter bearing only a single word in his son's hand: 'Lament.' Yi knew at once that Myeon was dead.

After their defeat at Myeongnyang, the Japanese sought revenge by attacking Yi's hometown in Asan. They set fire to his household and the entire village. Unable to endure the outrage, his twenty-one-year-old son Myeon rushed into the enemy and fell in battle. Yi, who had hoped that this brave and gifted son might one day succeed him, was left in inconsolable grief. In his War Diary he wrote:

"My entrails fell apart and I wept aloud.
How heartless is Heaven! My innards burn and are torn asunder.
It would be just if I had died and you had lived—
but you are gone and I remain. What greater injustice can there be?
The heavens are dark, and even the sun has changed its light."

In the annals of world naval warfare, the Battle of Myeongnyang stands among the most astonishing feats of command. Like Themistocles at Salamis, who crushed a far greater Persian fleet in the narrow straits of Greece, or Nelson at Trafalgar, who secured Britain's mastery of the seas against Napoleon, Yi Sun-sin at Myeongnyang defied impossible odds with only thirteen ships. Yet unlike those battles, where forces were at least comparable, Myeongnyang was fought against a disparity so vast that its outcome seems miraculous. Historians across the world regard it not merely as a victory of arms, but as a triumph of leadership, discipline, and the will of a people who refused to surrender their seas.

통곡
Lamentation

슬프다, 내 아들아!

나를 버리고 어디로 갔느냐

남달이 영특하기로 하늘이 세상에 두지 않는 것이냐

내가 지은 죄 때문에 앙화가 네 몸에 미친 것이냐

내 이제 세상에 살아있는들 누구에게 의지한단 말이냐

너를 따라 죽어 지하에서 같이 지내며 같이 울고 싶건만

네 형, 네 누이, 네 어머니가 의지 할 곳이 없으므로

아직은 참고 연명이나 한다마는

속은 다 썩고 형상만 남아 오직 울부짖을 따름이다

하룻밤 지내기가 1년 같구나

Alas, my son!

Why have you left me, and where have you gone?

Were you so gifted that Heaven could not suffer you in this world?

Was it my sins that drew this calamity upon your body?

Now that you are gone, whom have I left to lean upon?

I long to follow you, to die and dwell with you below the earth,

To weep beside you in the darkness.

Yet your brothers, your sister, your mother—

They have no one else to cling to,

So still I linger, though hollow in heart,

A husk that endures, a body that weeps.

Each night drags on like a year of sorrow,

And morning brings no end to grief.

노량해전
The Battle of Noryang

정유재란 당시 1598년 12월 16일 (선조 31년 음력 11월 19일) 이순신을 포함한 조명 연합 수군이 경상우도 남해현 노량해협에서 일본의 함대와 싸운 전투이다.

명량해전에서 대패한 일본군은 도독 유정과 진린이 이끄는 명나라 수군의 참전으로 남부 해상권이 조명 연합군으로 넘어가자, 해상 보급로를 차단당한 일본군은 고전을 면치 못한다. 더구나 1598년 도요토미 히데요시가 사망하자 조선 주둔 일본군의 수뇌부는 난관에 빠진다. 결국 일본군은 서둘러 전쟁을 끝내고 자국으로의 철군을 결정하고 순천, 사천, 울산 등지로 집결하며 철수를 서두른다. 순천 왜성에 주둔한 고니시 유키나가의 부대는 수차례의 순천 왜교성 전투로 고전하며 철수 퇴로가 차단되고 있었고, 이에 사천에 주둔 중이던 시마즈 요시히로, 고성에 주둔 중이던 다치바사 사케토리, 남해에 주둔 중이던 쇼 요시토시는 고니시 군을 구출하고, 본국으로 돌아갈 퇴로를 확보하기 위해 12월 15일 수군 6만여 명과 500여 척의 함선을 이끌고 노량으로 모인다.

이에 일본 함대가 노량을 통과할 것을 예측한 이순신은 명 수군은 남해도 죽도 뒤편에서 일본 수군의 퇴로를 차단케 하고, 자신은 순천 왜성의 고니시 봉쇄망을 풀고 남해도 서북단 관음포에 매복한다. 이후 12월 16일 새벽 4시경 요시히로등이 이끄는 일본 함선 500여 척이 노량에 진입한 후 조명 연합 함대와 치열한 전투를 벌이게 된다. 조선 수군은 도망가려는 왜군 전선을 완전히 소탕하기 위해 근접전을 벌이며 뒤쫓는다. 어둠이 서서히 걷혀가고 태양이 노량바다 동녘으로 떠오를 때 어디

선가 탄환이 날아와 이순신의 심장 언저리를 뚫고 지나간다. 이순신은 심장을 움켜 잡으며 "지금 싸움이 한창 급하니 내가 죽었다는 말을 알리지 마라."는 전령을 유언으로 남긴다.

장군의 뜻에 따라 슬픔에 복받친 장수는 이순신 장군의 갑옷을 입고 군사들을 독려하며 북을 친다. 그 소리가 온 바다를 뒤덮듯 우렁찼고 군사들의 사기는 휘날리는 대장기처럼 힘차고 당당했다. 왜군의 깃발들이 바닷속으로 들어가며 정오가 되어서야 전쟁이 끝이 났다. 화염이 검은 안개처럼 피어오르고 조선 수군들은 대장선으로 모여들었다.

이 전투로 350여 척의 일본 수군 전선이 파손되고 100여 척은 나포되며 겨우 50여 척만 살아남아 도주했다. 순천 왜성에 고립되었던 고니시도 겨우 탈출하여 노량해전에서 살아남은 군대와 함께 퇴각하였다고 전해진다. 이로써 노량해전과 정유재란이 막을 내리고 7년간의 긴 전쟁도 끝이 났다.

1598년 11월 19일 (선조 31년 양력 12월 16일) 나라를 구한 영웅이자 성웅 이순신 장군은 아득해지는 승리의 함성을 들으며 어느 때보다도 평온한 표정으로 향년 54세의 일기로 생을 마감한다.

On December 16, 1598 (lunar calendar: November 19, 31st year of King Seonjo), the combined Joseon–Ming fleet under Admiral Yi Sun-sin clashed with the retreating Japanese navy in the waters of Noryang, off Namhae.

After their catastrophic defeat at Myeongnyang, the Japanese had lost control of the southern seas to the allied fleets of Joseon and Ming. With their supply lines cut, their situation worsened. When news came that Toyotomi Hideyoshi had died in 1598, the Japanese high command resolved to end the war and retreat. They massed their forces at Suncheon, Sacheon, and Namhae to secure an escape route. Konishi Yukinaga, besieged at Suncheon fortress, faced collapse. To rescue him, Shimazu Yoshihiro, Tachibana Muneshige, and Shō Yoshitoshi gathered some 60,000 men and more than 500 warships at Noryang.

Anticipating this, Yi ordered the Ming fleet under Admiral Chen Lin (Jin Lin) to cut off the enemy's retreat from the east, while he himself broke the blockade of Suncheon and lay in wait at Gwaneumpo. In the early hours of December 16, as darkness still clung to the sea, the Japanese armada entered Noryang Strait. At 4 a.m., battle was joined. Cannon roared, arrows streaked the sky, and the waters erupted in fire and iron.

As dawn broke, Admiral Yi pressed the pursuit, driving his ships deep into the enemy. Then, amid the thunder of battle, a stray bullet struck near his heart. Clutching his wound, he gave his final command:
"The battle is at its height. Do not let my death be known."

Faithful to his order, his officers concealed their grief. One donned the Admiral's armor, beat the war drum, and rallied the men. The sound rolled across the sea like thunder, and the fleet fought with renewed fury. By noon, Japanese banners sank beneath the waves, their fleet shattered. Three hundred fifty enemy ships were destroyed, a hundred captured, and barely fifty limped away. Konishi escaped with remnants of his force, retreating at last from Joseon.

Thus ended the Battle of Noryang, the final clash of the Imjin Wars. And thus ended the seven years of war that had scourged the land.

On that day, November 19 of the lunar calendar (December 16, solar), the hero who had saved his nation, Admiral Yi Sun-sin, breathed his last. As the cries of victory resounded over the waters, he departed this world at the age of fifty-four—his face, it is said, calm and at peace.

스토리 전시
Story Exhibition

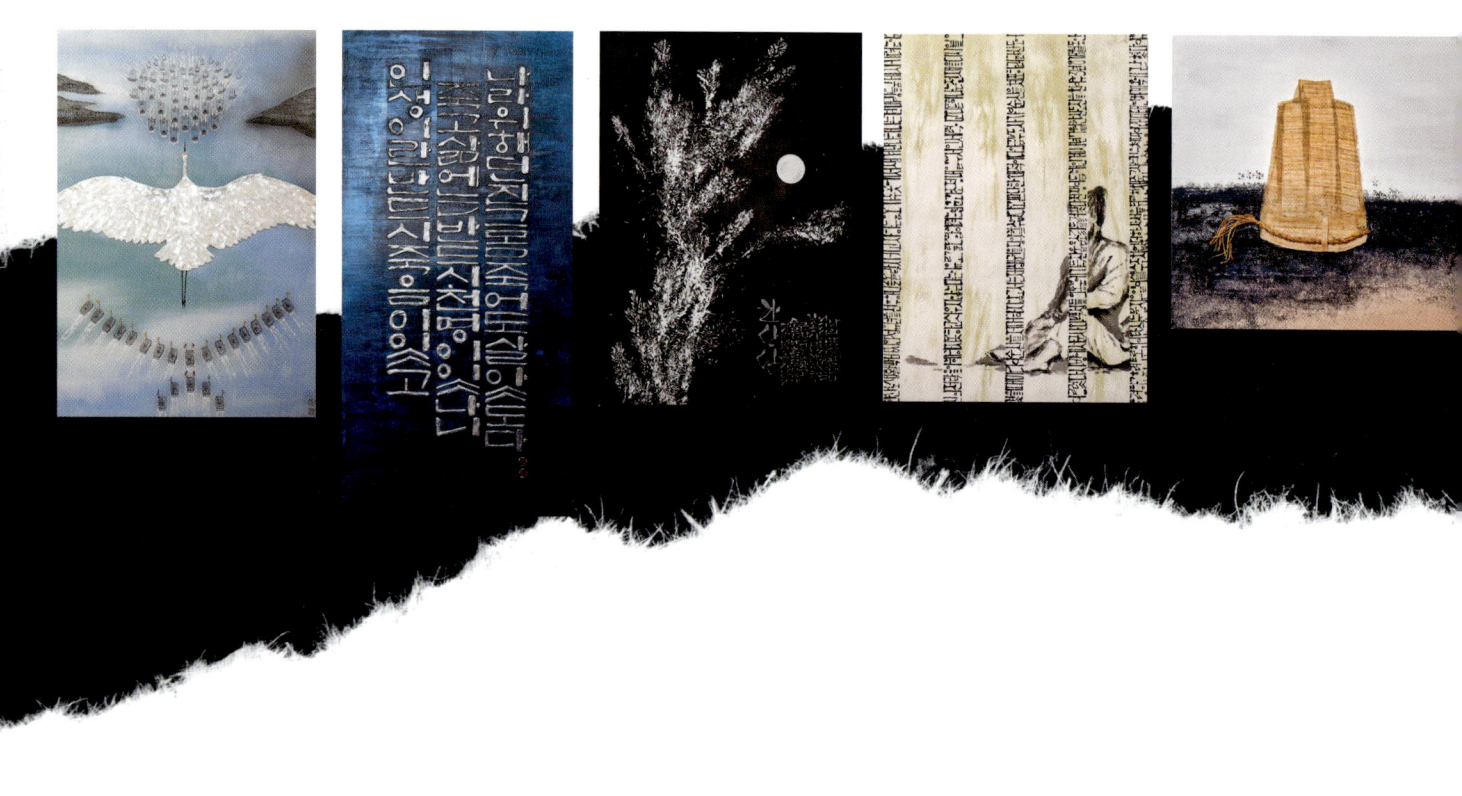

유산과 기억 : 성웅의 이야기

Legacy and Memory – Portrait of a Hero

이순신 장군 상
Admiral Yi Sun-sin: An Enduring Ideal

군자는

세상일을 두루 화합하되 시류에 따라 흐르지 않는다.

윗자리에 있을 땐 교만하지 않고, 아래 일을 할 때에는 윗사람을 거스리지 않는다.

국가로 부터 영화를 얻더라도 궁색할 때의 마음을 잊지 않고, 국가가 혼란스러우면 설사 죽음에 이르더라도 나라에 대한 지조에 변함이 없어야 한다.

묻기를 좋아하고, 사소한 일도 자세히 살펴 일과 이치에 막힘이 없도록 깊이 연구한다.

목표 삼은 일을 실천해 가던 중 어려움이 생겼다 해도 결코 중간에 그만두지 않는다.

옳고 바른 일을 하는데 세상이 몰라준다 해도 후회하거나 서운해 하지 않는다.

남을 상대할 때 허물은 숨겨주고 내 몸에 베풀어 보아서 싫을 일은 강요하지 말아야 한다.

언행이 일치해야 하니 항상 말이 행동에 부합되는지를 살피고, 행동에 앞서 자신이 한 말을 되돌아보아야 한다.

위로 하늘을 원망하지 말고 아래로 사람을 탓하지 말아야 한다.

자신의 분수에 맞게 처신함으로써 어떠한 처지에 있더라도 편할 수 있어야 한다.

The Way of the Noble Man

He harmonizes with all affairs of the world, yet does not drift with the tide of fashion.

In high office he is never arrogant; in lowly duty he does not oppose his superiors.

Even when he gains honor from the state, he does not forget the heart he had in poverty; when the nation falls into chaos, he remains loyal to it even unto death.

He delights in asking questions, examines even the smallest matters, and studies deeply so that no task or principle remains obscure.

When pursuing his chosen path, he does not abandon it midway, even when difficulties arise.

If he does what is right and just, he feels no regret nor bitterness even if the world fails to recognize him.

In dealing with others, he conceals their faults and never forces upon others what he himself would find hateful.

His words and deeds are as one: he ensures that his speech accords with his actions, and before acting, he reflects upon what he has said.

He does not resent Heaven above, nor does he blame others below.

By conducting himself according to his proper measure, he finds ease in any station of life.

역사는 흐른다 *History flows on*

한글로 그리는 '성웅 이순신 장군의 일대기'를 작업하며, 이순신 장군의 나라와 백성을 향한 헌신적인 사랑, 사사로운 욕심에 얽매이지 않고 불의와 타협하지 않는 올곧은 성품, 절망 속에서도 포기하지 않는 의지, 뛰어난 지략과 통찰력, 유비무환의 자세, 창의적인 전술, 엄격한 군율로 군의 기강을 잡고 동시에 부하들을 보살피는 인간적인 면모, 부하들의 공을 인정하며 소통하는 엄격하나 인자한 리더십, 전쟁 중에도 어머니의 안부를 끊임없이 살피는 지극한 효심, 이러한 덕목이 위기의 시대에서 나라를 구할 수 있었던 정신이었으리라.

오늘 우리에게 귀감이 되는 이순신 장군과 조일 전쟁을 승리로 이끈 사람들의 충심과 헌신에 감사하며, 마지막 작품은 새벽 바다, 동이 틀 무렵을 배경으로 삼는다.

장군은 방패에 가려져 있고
슬픔에 복받친 장수가 북을 친다
그 소리가 바다를 채우자
화염이 안개처럼 피어오르고
붉고 푸른 깃발이 희미하나,
선명하게 드러난다

일출이 애도하듯 그를 감싸며
무어라 말을 하는 듯 보인다

우리는 그 말이 무엇인지를 안다

In portraying the life of Admiral Yi Sun-sin through the letters of Hangul, we encounter the essence of a man whose devotion to his nation and people knew no bounds. He lived without succumbing to selfish ambition, never compromising with injustice, and upheld integrity even in despair. His unwavering will, keen insight, and readiness for all contingencies; his inventive strategies and tactical brilliance; his strict discipline tempered by compassion for his men; his recognition of merit and open communication; his stern yet humane leadership; and his filial devotion—inquiring after his mother even in the midst of war—these were the virtues that enabled him to save his country in an age of peril.

Today, we honor Admiral Yi and those who fought beside him, whose loyalty and sacrifice carried Joseon to victory in the Imjin War. To them we give thanks. And so, the final scene is set upon the dawn sea, at the breaking of day.

The Admiral, hidden behind his shield;
A grieving officer strikes the drum.
Its sound fills the sea,
As flames rise like mist,
And crimson and azure banners emerge—
Dim, yet radiant.

The rising sun, as if in mourning enfolds him in its light, as though it speaks a final word.

And we know well what that word is.

바람이 바뀔 수도 있겠습니다

Perhaps the wind may yet change.

당신의 크기를 정합니다

I set the measure of your magnitude.

밤새 늘려 놓았던 크기를
눈을 뜨자마자 줄입니다
보기에는 좋으나 세밀함이 사라져서
다시 조금씩 키웁니다

Through the night I stretched your size,
yet at dawn I fold it back.
It looks pleasing, but the fine lines vanish,
so I grow it again, little by little.

사이가 좁혀집니다
좁아진 면은 여백을 가져가고,

The spaces draw closer;
what narrows, steals away the margin.

당신의 바다를 줄입니다
사람들을 뺍니다
한 시절이 날아가 버리고
풍랑이 사라집니다

I shrink your sea,
I take the people out,
an age takes flight,
and the storm subsides.

사라진 곳에서는 상상이 자라나지요

From the hollowed space, imagination begins to sprout.

책을 보면서 칼을 생각하고
칼을 만지면서 책을 생각하고
달을 보면서 그리워한 것은
다른 무엇일 수도 있겠습니다

Reading a book, I think of the sword.
Touching the sword, I think of the book.
Longing at the moon,
perhaps it was for something else.

상상을 넣지는 않을거예요
역사화는 사실을 담아야 하니까
풀 바람 하늘은 바뀔 수도 있겠습니다
비가 올 수도 아이가 자랄 수도 있겠습니다
시간은 흘러가므로
흘러서
여기에 와 닿으므로

I will not weave in imagination—
for history painting must cradle truth.
The grass, the wind, the sky may change;
rain may fall, a child may grow.
Time flows,
and flowing,
arrives here.

다시 생각합니다
크기를 줄이니 세밀함이 사라지고
부분을 빼니 이야기가 끊기는,
당신을 생각하면 온 우주를 채워도 부족하지만
이 땅은 너무 좁고 이 장은 너무 작습니다

정해진 곳에 놓으려 하니
당신이 머리를 숙일 것 같고
넓은 곳에 놓으려 하니
초라해질 것 같아서

다시 크기를 잽니다

Again, I measure.

When I lessen the size, the detail is lost.

When I subtract the parts, the story breaks.

To think of you—

even the universe cannot contain enough.

Yet this land feels too narrow,

this page too small.

If I set you in a fixed place,

you might bow your head.

If I set you in a vast one,

you might look diminished.

So once more,

I measure your magnitude.

작가 서미숙, Mi-Sook Seo

부록 : 그를 기리며

Appendix – In Commemoration of Admiral Yi

이순신 장군에 대한 국내외 주요 인사의 평가
Voices Across History : Evaluations of Admiral Yi Sun-sin

정조 (조선 22대 임금) King Jeongjo (22nd King of Joseon)

정조는 "나의 선조께서 나라를 다시 일으킨 공로의 기초는 오직 충무공 한 분의 힘에 의함이다."라고 말하며 이순신을 성군(聖君)인 세종대왕과 더불어 조선의 중흥을 이끈 위대한 인물로 평가했습니다. 그는 200여 년간 제대로 조명받지 못했던 이순신의 업적을 재조명하고, 그의 행록(行錄)을 편찬하는 등 국가적 차원에서 충무공을 기리는 사업을 주도했습니다.

King Jeongjo declared: "The foundation of my ancestor's restoration of the nation rests solely upon the power of Admiral Yi." He placed Yi alongside King Sejong the Great, recognizing him as one of the greatest figures in Joseon's resurgence. Jeongjo took the lead in honoring Yi at the national level, compiling his official records and restoring the memory of a hero neglected for nearly two centuries.

조선왕조실록 (사관의 논평) Annals of the Joseon Dynasty (Scribes' Commentary)

"이순신은 사람됨이 충용(忠勇)하고 재략(才略)도 있었으며, 기율(紀律)을 밝히고 군졸을 사랑하니 사람들이 모두 즐겨 따랐다." 실록의 사관은 이순신 장군의 죽음을 기록하며 그의 인품과 능력, 그리고 부하들에게서 받는 신뢰를 높이 평가했습니다. 또한, 조정이 그를 제대로 대우하지 못해 나라가 위기를 겪었음을 한탄하기도 했습니다.

The court historians wrote: "Yi Sun-sin was loyal and brave, possessed of talent and strategy. He upheld strict discipline while caring for his soldiers, and thus all followed him gladly." They lamented that the court had failed to value him properly, and that such neglect had brought peril to the nation.

유성룡 (조선 영의정) Yu Seong-ryong (Chief State Councillor of Joseon)

"이순신은 평소 말수가 적고 근엄하여 군중에서는 우러러보지 않는 사람이 없었다. 그리고 매사에 신중하여 작은 것도 소홀히 하지 않았다." 징비록(懲毖錄)의 저자인 유성룡은 이순신을 발탁한 인물로서 그의 뛰어난 재능과 인품을 누구보다 잘 알고 있었습니다. 그는 이순신을 군사적 천재이자 도덕적 완벽에 가까운 인물로 평가했습니다.

Yu, who first recommended Yi for command and authored the Jingbirok (Book of Corrections), observed: "Yi Sun-sin spoke little and carried himself with dignity, so that in the camp none failed to revere him. He was cautious in all matters, neglecting nothing, however small." To Yu, Yi was both a military genius and a man of near-perfect moral integrity.

신채호 (역사학자, 독립운동가) Shin Chae-ho (Historian and Independence Activist)

신채호 선생은 일제강점기 당시 '조선상고사' 등에서 이순신 장군을 '조선민족사의 위대한 영웅'으로 묘사하며 민족주의 사학의 관점에서 그의 위대함을 강조했습니다. 그는 이순신의 상무정신(尙武精神)과 자주적 정신을 통해 민족적 자긍심을 고취시키려 했습니다.

During the Japanese occupation, Shin described Yi as 'a great hero in the history of the Korean people' in his works such as Joseon Sanggosa (Early History of Joseon). From a nationalist perspective, he emphasized Yi's martial spirit (sangmu jeongsin) and independence of will, holding him up as a source of national pride.

김구 (독립운동가) Kim Gu (Independence Leader)

김구 선생은 이순신 장군을 '나라의 위기를 극복한 위대한 선조'로 존경했습니다. 특히 대한민국 임시정부 시절, 나라 잃은 백성들에게 이순신 장군의 정신을 본받아 나라를 되찾아야 한다고 강조하며 이순신을 독립운동의 정신적 지주로 삼았습니다.

Kim Gu revered Yi as 'a great forebear who saved the nation in its hour of crisis.' During the Provisional Government period, he urged the Korean people to embody Yi's spirit in their own struggle for independence, regarding him as a spiritual pillar of the movement.

도고 헤이하치로 (일본 해군 제독) Togo Heihachiro (Japanese Admiral, Hero of the Russo-Japanese War)

러일전쟁의 영웅으로 칭송받던 도고 헤이하치로는 "나를 영국의 넬슨 제독에 비교하는 것은 가능하나, 조선의 이순신 장군에게 비교하는 것은 황송한 일이다. 이순신 장군은 국가의 지원 없이 홀로 싸운 장수이며, 해군 역사에서 군신(軍神)이라 부를 수 있는 사람은 오직 이순신 장군 한 사람뿐이다."라고 말했습니다.

Often hailed as 'Japan's Nelson,' Admiral Tōgō humbly remarked: "It may be possible to compare me with Admiral Nelson of England, but to compare me with Admiral Yi Sun-sin of Joseon would be presumptuous. Admiral Yi fought without the support of his state, and in all naval history, he alone may rightly be called the God of War at Sea."

조지 알렉산더 발라드 (영국 해군 소장) George Alexander Ballard (Rear Admiral, Royal Navy, UK)

영국 해군대학 교관이자 전략가였던 발라드는 "이순신은 트라팔가 해전의 영웅인 넬슨 제독에 필적하는 인물"이라고 평가하며, 이순신의 전략적 천재성을 높이 샀습니다. 그는 이순신 장군을 '아시아의 넬슨'이라 부르기도 했습니다.

Ballard, strategist and instructor at the Royal Naval College, praised Yi as "a commander equal to Nelson of Trafalgar." He admired Yi's strategic genius, calling him 'the Nelson of Asia.'

앨프레드 마한 (미국 해군 제독) Alfred Thayer Mahan (U.S. Naval Admiral, Father of Sea Power Theory)

'해양력의 창시자'로 불리는 마한 제독은 이순신 장군의 전략을 연구하며 "이순신은 나폴레옹과 더불어 세계 군사사에서 가장 위대한 전략가 중 한 명"이라고 평가했습니다.

Mahan studied Yi's campaigns and judged: "Yi Sun-sin ranks with Napoleon among the greatest strategists in military history." He regarded Yi's naval operations as timeless lessons in the art of war.

이순신 장군의 생애와 연보
Chronology of Yi Sun-sin's Life

년도/Year	사건/Major events		나이/Age
1545	한성부 건천동(현 서울 중구 인현동)에서 출생 아산 외가로 이사 (10~12세쯤으로 추정)	Born in Geoncheon-dong, Hanseong (modern Inhyeon-dong, Jung-gu, Seoul). Moved to his maternal home in Asan.	Est. 10-12
1565	보성 군수 방진의 딸과 결혼	Married the daughter of Bang Jin, magistrate of Boseong.	Age 21
1567 - 02 1571 - 02	맏아들 회 태어남 둘째아들 울 태어남	First son Hoe born. Second son Yeol born.	Age 23 Age 27
1572 - 08	훈련원 별과 시험에 응시했으나 말에서 낙마	Attempted the Military Service Examination, fell from his horse.	Age 28
1576 - 02 - 12	식년 무과에 병과로 급제 함경도 동구비보 권관으로 첫 부임	Passed the national military examination First post as a junior officer in Hamgyeong Province.	Age 32
1579	훈련원 봉사 충청병사 군관	Appointed to the Training Bureau; later assigned to Chungcheong forces.	Age 35
1580 - 07	전라좌수영의 발포 수군만호	Posted as naval commander (Manho) at Balpo in Jeolla Province.	Age 36
1581 - 12	군기 경차관 서익의 모함으로 파직	Dismissed due to false charges by Inspector Seo Ik.	Age 37
1582 - 05	훈련원 봉사로 복직	Reinstated as officer of the Training Bureau.	Age 38
1583 - 07 - 10 - 11 - 11	함경도 남경사 군관 건원보(함경도 경원내) 군관 훈련원 참군으로 승진 부친(향년 73세) 사망	Service in Hamgyeong. Promoted to Captain. Father passed away at age 73.	Age 39
1586 - 01	사복시 주부 조산보 만호	Appointed to Sa-bok-si and as commander at Josanbo.	Age 42
1587 - 08 - 10	녹둔도 둔전관 겸함 이일에 의해 파직, 첫 번째 백의종군	Appointed commander at Nokdun-do Falsely accused and dismissed; first service in 'white robes'.	Age 43
1588 - 01	여진족 정벌 공으로 백의종군 해제	Restored to office after campaign against the Jurchens.	Age 44
1589 - 01 - 11 - 12	전라관찰사 이광의 군관 겸 전라도 조방장 선전관 겸함 정읍현감	Appointed county magistrate of Jeongeup; served in various posts.	Age 45

1591 - 02	유성룡의 추천으로 전라좌수사에 임명, 거북선 건조	Recommended by Yu Seong-ryong; appointed Commander of the Left Jeolla Navy; construction of the Turtle Ship.	Age 47
1592 - 04	임진왜란 발발	Imjin War begins	Age 48
- 05	옥포, 합포 적진포해전 연전 연승, 사천해전에서 거북선 처음 사용	Yi leads Joseon Navy to repeated victories at Okpo, Sacheon (first deployment of Turtle Ship)	
- 06	당포 당항포 율포해전 연승- 자헌 대부에 승자	Victory at Dangpo, Promoted to Jauhon Daebu	
- 07	견내량, 안골포해전 연승- 정헌대부 승진	Consecutive victories at Gyeonnaeryang and Angolpo (promoted to Jeongheon Daebu)	
- 09	부산포해전, 정운 장군 정사	Battle of Busan Harbor (death of General Jeong Woon)	
1593 - 03	웅포해전	Battle of Ungpo	Age 49
- 07	본영을 여수에서 한산도로 옮김	Moved fleet headquarters to Hansando; appointed	
- 08	산도수군통제사로 임명, 조선 수군 총괄	Samdo Sugun Tongjesa (Commander of the Three Provinces Navy).	
1594 - 03	3월, 2차 당항포 해전 승	Further victories at Danghangpo	Age 50
- 09	1차 장문포에서 왜선 2척 분멸 2차 장문포해전 승	First Victory at Jangmunpo. Second Victory at Jangmunpo.	
1595 - 01	맏아들 회 혼례	Eldest son Hoe [hwe] marries.	Age 51
1597	가등청장이 온다는 허위 정보에 출전하지 않음	Withheld action on false intelligence	Age 53
1597 - 02	조정과 원균의 모함으로 서울로 압송	Wrongly accused and imprisoned due to	
- 03	옥에 갇힘	intrigues by the Joseon Court and Won Gyun	
- 04	정탁의 신구차로 특사됨, 두 번째 백의종군	Released and ordered to serve again in white robes.	
	모친상(향년 83세), 해암 바닷가에서 유해 봉견	Mother passed away at age of 83	
- 06	초계의 도원수 권율로 들어감	Joined Commander-in-Chief Gwon Yul in Chogye	
- 07	왜적의 기습으로 원균 패사, 칠전량해전 패망	Won Gyun's disastrous defeat at Chilcheollyang	
- 08	삼도수군통제사로 재임명, 벽파진에 진영 설치	Reinstated as Commander	
- 09	명량해전 대승 (조선 전선 13척: 일본 전선 133척 이상)	Secured decisive victory at the Battle of Myeongnyang with only 13 ships.	
- 10	아산 고향 방화, 명량해전 패배로 왜군 보복, 대항하던 셋째 아들 면 사망	Home in Asan burned in Japanese reprisal; third son Myeon killed while resisting.	
1598 - 02	고금도로 진영을 옮기고 경작하여 군비 강화	Strengthened forces at Geogeumdo	Age 54
- 07	명나라 진린과 연합작전 시행 절이도 해전에서 송여종이 적선 6척과 머리 69급 포획 (진린에게 줌)	Allied with Ming Admiral Chen Lin. Song Yeo-jong captured 6 enemy ships and 69 heads, later presented to Admiral Chen Lin.	
- 11	노량해전에서 승리를 이끌던 중 전사 유언 "나의 죽음을 적에게 알리지 말라"	November, fell in battle at Noryang, leaving the command: "Do not let my death be known."	

1604	선조/ 선무공신 1등에 추봉되고 덕풍부원군에 추증	Posthumously enshrined as First Rank Meritorious Subject; titled Duke of Deokpung.	-
1613	광해/ 충열사, 충민사, 현충사에 배향	Enshrined at memorial shrines	-
1643	인조/ '충무' 시호 받음	Bestowed the posthumous title 'Chungmu' (Loyal Valor).	-
179	정조/ 7월, 영의정에 추증	King Jeongjo posthumously elevated him to Chief State Councillor.	-

용어집
Glossary

한글	설명	Revised Romanization of Korean	Definition
거북선	세계 최초의 갑판 덮개식 전투함. 용머리·쇠못 장착, 근접·포격전 특화	Geobukseon	Turtle Ship The world's first ironclad warship; used in naval battles with features such as iron spikes, cannon, and ramming tactics.
군율	조선 수군을 유지한 엄격한 군사 규율	Gunnyul	Military Discipline
녹둔도	군량 생산 둔전이 있던 곳. 1587년 전투로 유명	Nokdun-do	Nokdun-do Island An island with military farmlands for grain production; famous for the 1587 battle.
난중일기	이순신 장군이 전쟁 중 기록한 일기. 세계기록유산	Nanjung Ilgi	War Diary Admiral Yi Sun-sin's war diary; registered in UNESCO's Memory of the World.
둔전	군량 확보를 위한 국영 농토. 녹둔도 사건 관련	Dunjeon	Military Farmland related to Nokdun-do Island
백의종군	파직된 관원이 벼슬 없이 흰옷 차림으로 전장에 따르는 형벌·충절	Baekui Jonggun	Service in White Robes Punishment where an official, stripped of office, served the army in plain clothes while retaining the status of a former officer.
삼도수군통제사	충청·전라·경상 3도 수군을 총괄한 최고 지휘관	Samdo Sugun Tongjesa	Commander of the Three Provinces Navy Supreme commander of the naval forces of Chungcheong, Jeolla, and Gyeongsang provinces.
선조	조선 제14대 왕 (재위 1567~1608). 임진왜란 시기 군주	Seonjo	King Seonjo The 14th king of Joseon (reigned 1567-1608). Ruler during the Imjin War.
유비무환	『서경』 유래. "미리 준비하면 근심이 없다"는 뜻	Yubi Muhwan	Preparedness Prevents Peril Confucian saying: "If you are prepared, you will have no worries." Used by Yi Sun-sin.
임진왜란	1592~1593년 일본의 1차 침략 전쟁	Imjin Waeran	Imjin War Japanese invasions of Korea from 1592-1593, the first invasion.
정유재란	1597~1598년 일본의 2차 침략 전쟁	Jeongyu Jaeran	The second Japanese invasion from 1597-1598.
정조	조선 제22대 왕. 이순신을 재평가·기념사업 주도	Jeongjo	King Jeongjo The 22nd king of Joseon; honored Yi Sun-sin by compiling records and memorial projects.

충무공	1643년 인조가 내린 이순신의 시호	Chungmugong	Lord of Loyal Valor Posthumous title granted in 1643 under King Injo to Admiral Yi Sun-sin.
충효	임금에 대한 충성과 부모에 대한 효도. 이순신의 인격 핵심	Chung-Hyo	Loyalty and Filial Piety Confucian virtue of loyalty to the king and filial duty to parents; reflected in Yi Sun-sin's life.
판옥선	조선 수군의 주력 전선. 화포·기동에 탁월	Panokseon	Multi-deck Warship Joseon's main warship, a sturdy multi-deck vessel used in naval battles.
필사즉생 필생즉사	명량해전 전 훈시. 죽음을 각오해야 살 수 있다는 뜻	Pilsajiksaeng, Pilsaengjiksa	To Seek Death Is to Find Life Famous wartime maxim: "If you seek death, you shall live; if you seek life, you shall die." by Admiral Yi Sun-sin

참고문헌
Reference

난중일기 노승석역 도서출팜 여해

징비록 유성룡, 이재호역, 위즈덤 하우스

중용 동양고전연구회, 민음사

이순신 김종대, 시루

임진왜란 임용한, 레드리버

이순신 김산호, 한울

충무공 이순신전서 박기봉, 비봉 출판사

이순신과 임진왜란 이순신 역사 연구회

Yi, Sun-sin. **Nanjung Ilgi (War Diary of Admiral Yi Sun-sin)**. Translated by Seung-seok Noh. Yehae Publishing.

Yu, Seong-ryong. **Jingbirok (Book of Corrections).** Translated by Jae-ho Lee. Wisdom House.

*The Classic of the Mean (Zhongyong). East Asian Classics Research Association. Minumsa Publishing.

Kim, Jong-dae. **Yi Sun-sin.** Siru Publishing.

Im, Yong-han. **The Imjin War**. Red River Publishing.

Kim, San-ho. **Yi Sun-sin.** Hanul Publishing.

Pak, Gi-bong. **The Complete Works of Admiral Yi Sun-sin (Chungmugong Jeonse)**. Bibong Publishing.

Yi Sun-sin Historical Research Association. **Yi Sun-sin and the Imjin War.**

바람이 바뀔 수도 있겠습니다

서미숙

한글 문화예술 명인
(한글조형아트부문 제24-06-07-11호)
시인 (필명 서이교)
캘리그라퍼 (아호 예송)
무궁화 서화대전 심사위원
전 세계태권도연맹 시범단 연출감독
한글아트 '아토' 대표

저서
2025	성웅 이순신, 한글로 기억되다
2020	캘리에세이 엄마꽃

전시
2025.10	서울 중구, 이순신 장군 탄생 480주년 기념 특별전 (중구청 로비)
2025.09	중구문화원 개원30주년 특별 초대전ㅣ세종과 이순신의 만남 (중구문화원 예문갤러리)
2025.02	올해의 작가 100인 초대전 2025 (중구문화원 예문갤러리)
2024.07	13회 한국문화명인, 명인청구전 (한국예총극장, 명인 갤러리)
2024.06	캘리에세이 개인전 솔로몬의 지혜 '모든 일에 때가 있다 (극동방송 갤러리)
2024.04	프랑스 파리 올림픽 개최 기념 전시회 (VOUS ETES RECOMPENSES)
2023.08	手作 그룹전 (인사동 갤러리라메르)
2023.07	기독교 환경단체 녹색교회 캠페인 기획초대 개인전 (광림교회 전시실)
2022.01	올해의 작가 100인 초대전 2022 (인사동 한국관)
2020.11	캘리에세이 '엄마꽃' 출판기념 전시회 개인전 (인사동 아카데미갤러리)
2020.02	올해의 작가 100인 초대전 2020 (인사동 인사아트프라자)
2019.09	心, 물들다 서미숙 개인전 (극동방송갤러리)
2019.08	에너지의 날 기획초대 개인전 '물의 노래' (청주 국제 에코 콤플렉스)
2019.05	캘리에세이 개인전 '시간여행' (갤러리 마을)
2019.02	이탈리아 로마 신년 초대전 (ISTITUTO CULTU RALE COREANA DI ROMA)
2019.02	올해의 작가 100인 초대전 2019 (대한미협 갤러리예술공간)
2019.10	예藝 이음 독거노인돕기 자선 전시회 '마음 스미다' (극동방송 갤러리)
2018.11	예藝 이음 독거 노인 돕기 자선 전시회 '길을 찾아서' (극동방송 갤러리)
2016~2023	글향 회원전

수상
2024.04	프랑스 파리 올림픽 개최 기념 전시회 평론가 상
2022.02	올해의 작가 100인 초대전 대상 한국미술협회 이사장상
2019.10	무궁화 서화대전 초대작가상

2019.07	한글 서예대전 (월간 서예) 특선
2018.10	대한민국 단군 서예 대전 특선
2018.08	한글 서예 협회 서울지부 서예대전 현대서예 특선
2018.06	한글 서예대전 (월간 서예) 특선
2018.06	대한민국 남북통일 예술협회 세계환경예술대전 금상
2018.04	무궁화 서화대전 우수상
2018.03	한글 서예협회 인천지회 서예대전 현대서예 특선

세계 태권도 연맹 시범단 연출작품

2023.02	UAE 오픈 세계 태권도 대회 개막식/ 푸자이라
2022.11	과달라하라 태권도 선수권 대회 개막식/ 멕시코
2022.10	미국 NBC 아메리카 갓 탈렌트 올스타전/ LA
2022.06	이태리 시티투어/ 밀라노외 6개 도시
2022.04	고양시 세계 품새대회 개막식/ 한국
2022.01	푸자이라 오픈 세계대회 개막식/ 아랍에미레이트
2022.01	세계 태권도 우먼스대회 개막식/ 사우디아라비아
2021.10	프랑스 갓 탈렌트 방송/ 파리
2021.08	미국 NBC 아메리카 갓 탈렌트 본선 결선/ 허리우드
2021.04	미국 NBC 아메리카 갓 탈렌트 예선/ 허리우드
2020.02	인도 문화의날 축하공연/ 인도 콜카타
2020.01	UAE 오픈 세계대회 개막식/ 푸자이라
2019.10	불가리아 시티투어
2019.09	중국 전국 청소년 체육대회 개막식/ 중국 호남성
2019.09	이탈리아 갓 탈렌트 방송/ 이탈리아
2019.05	이태리 시티투어/ 나폴리 외 6개 도시
2019.05	멘체스터 세계 태권도 선수권 대회 개막식/ 영국
2019.04	UN 본부 초청 남북합동공연/ 스위스 제네바
2019.04	IOC(국제올림픽조직원회)초청 올림픽박물관 남북 합동공연/ 스위스 로잔
2019.04	ITF(북측태권도 시범단)본부 초청 남북 합동공연/ 오스트리아
2019.01	푸자이라 오픈 세계대회 개막식/ 아랍에미레이트
2019.12	세계 그랜드 슬램 개막식/ 중국 우시
2018.11	남북태권도 합동공연/ 평양
2018.06	교황청 초청공연/ 로마, 바티칸시국
2018.04	평창 동계 올림픽 남북 태권도 합동 개막식 식전공연/ 한국
2017.06	무주 세계태권도 선수권대회 개막식/ 한국
2016.08	리우데자네이루 하계 올림픽 개막식/ 브라질
2015.05	첼라빈스크 세계태권도 선수권대회/ 러시아

SEO MI SOOK

Master of Korean Hangeul Culture and Arts
(Hangeul Formative Art, No. 24-06-07-11)
Poet (pen name Seo I-gyo)
Calligrapher (art name Yesong)
Jury Member, National Mugunghwa Calligraphy Exhibition
Director & Producer, World Taekwondo Demonstration Team
Founder & CEO, Hangeul Art ATO

Publications
2025	'Sacred Hero Yi Sun-sin, Remembered in the Letters of Hangul'
2020	Calli-Essay: 'Mother Flower'

Exhibitions
2025.10	Seoul Jung-gu, Special Exhibition Commemorating the 480th Anniversary of Admiral Yi Sun-sin's Birth (Jung-gu Office Lobby)
2025.09	Jung-gu Cultural Center 30th Anniversary Exhibition | The Meeting of Sejong and Yi Sun-sin (Yemun Gallery, Jung-gu Cultural Center)
2025.02	100 Artists of the Year 2025 (Korean Hall, Insa-dong)
2024.07	13th Korean Masters' Exhibition, Cheonggu Hall (Korea Art Association Theater & Gallery)
2024.06	Solo Exhibition, 'There Is a Time for Everything' (Far East Broadcasting Gallery)
2024.04	Paris Olympic Commemorative Exhibition, France (VOUS ETES RECOMPENSES)
2023.08	Handmade Group Exhibition (Insa-dong Gallery La Mer, Seoul)
2023.07	Solo Invitation Exhibition for Green Church Environmental Campaign (Seoul)
2022.01	100 Artists of the Year (Korean Hall, Insa-dong)
2020.11	Solo Exhibition, 'Mother Flower' (Academy Gallery, Insa-dong)
2020.02	100 Artists of the Year 2020 (Korean Hall, Insa-dong)
2019.09	Solo Exhibition, 'Heart, Stained with Color' (Far East Broadcasting Gallery)
2019.08	Song of Water, Environmental Exhibition (Cheongju International Eco-Complex)
2019.05	Solo Exhibition, 'Time Travel' (Gallery Maeul, Seoul)
2019.02	New Year Invitational Exhibition (Korean Cultural Center, Rome, Italy)
2019.02	100 Artists of the Year 2019 (Korean Hall, Insa-dong)
2019.10	Charity Exhibition, 'Heart Embracing the Lonely' (Far East Broadcasting Gallery)
2018.11	Charity Exhibition, 'Finding the Way' (Far East Broadcasting Gallery)
2016~2023	Annual Member Exhibitions (Geulhyang Calligraphy Society)

Awards

2024.04	Critics' Prize, Paris Olympic Commemorative Exhibition
2022.02	Grand Prize, 100 Artists of the Year (Korean Fine Arts Association Chairman's Award)
2019.10	Invitational Artist Award, Mugunghwa Calligraphy Exhibition
2019.07	Special Prize, Korean Hangeul Calligraphy Exhibition (Monthly Calligraphy)
2018.10	Special Prize, National Dangun Calligraphy Exhibition
2018.08	Special Prize, Korean Hangeul Calligraphy Exhibition (Seoul Branch)
2018.06	Gold Prize, World Environmental Art Exhibition (Korea Association for Inter-Korean Unification Arts)
2018.06	Special Prize, Korean Hangeul Calligraphy Competition (Monthly Seoye)
2018.04	Excellence Award, Mugunghwa Calligraphy Exhibition

World Taekwondo Demonstration Team - Direction & Productions

2023.02	UAE Open World Taekwondo Championships (Fujairah, UAE)
2022.11	World Taekwondo Championships (Guadalajara, Mexico)
2022.10	America's Got Talent: All Stars (Los Angeles, USA)
2022.06	City Tour of Italy (Milan and 6 other cities)
2022.04	World Taekwondo Poomsae Championships (Goyang, Korea)
2022.01	Opening Ceremony, Fujairah Open World Taekwondo Championships (UAE)
2022.01	Opening Ceremony, World Taekwondo Women's Championships (Saudi Arabia)
2021.10	France's Got Talent (Paris, France)
2021.08	America's Got Talent Finals (Hollywood, USA)
2021.04	America's Got Talent Semi-Finals (Hollywood, USA)
2020.02	Indian Cultural Day (Kolkata, India)
2020.01	Opening Ceremony, UAE Open World Championships (Fujairah)
2019.10	City Tour (Bulgaria)
2019.09	Opening Ceremony, China National Youth Sports Games (Hunan, China)
2019.09	Italia's Got Talent (Italy)
2019.05	City Tour, Italy (Naples and 6 other cities)
2019.05	Opening Ceremony, Manchester World Taekwondo Championships (United Kingdom)
2019.04	Joint North-South Taekwondo Performance, UN Headquarters (Geneva, Switzerland)
2019.04	IOC Olympic Museum Joint Performance (Lausanne, Switzerland)
2019.04	Joint North-South Taekwondo Performance, Invitation by ITF Headquarters (Austria)
2019.01	Opening Ceremony, Fujairah Open World Championships (United Arab Emirates)
2019.12	Opening Ceremony, World Grand Slam (Wuxi, China)
2018.11	Joint North-South Taekwondo Performance (Pyongyang, North Korea)
2018.06	Vatican Invitation Performance (Rome, Vatican City)
2018.04	Opening Ceremony Performance, PyeongChang Winter Olympics (Korea)
2017.06	Opening Ceremony, Muju World Taekwondo Championships (Korea)
2016.08	Rio de Janeiro Summer Olympics (Brazil)
2015.05	2015 World Taekwondo Championships (Chelyabinsk, Russia)

성웅 이순신, 한글로 기억되다

초판 1쇄 발행 2025년 09월 18일

지은이 서미숙
펴낸이 김형준
펴낸곳 예모이
등록번호 제25100-2025-000077호
번역 Jessica Kim
주소 서울 성동구 금호로 15 118-104
전화 010-3364-6073
홈페이지 www.yemoi.co.kr
이메일 yemoi@yemoi.co.kr

ISBN 979-11-994588-0-2 (03640)

값 28,000원